REAL LABOU

The biography of Dennis Turner,
Bilston steel workers' leader,
co-operator, Wolverhampton councillor,
member of parliament, and
peer of the realm

by Frank Reeves and Mel Chevannes

following a series of interviews
in December 2013 and January 2014
with Dennis Turner, and his family,
friends, and colleagues

*'The banner bright, the symbol plain*
*Of human right and human gain'*

# BLUE ROOF BOOKS

Published in 2014 by Blue Roof Books, 53 Woodthorne Road, Tettenhall, Wolverhampton, WV6 8TU.

Copyright © Frank Reeves and Mel Chevannes, 2014.

ISBN 978-0-9570042-1-4

In affectionate memory of Dennis Turner, a loyal comrade and friend, and peerless champion of the common people of Bilston, Wolverhampton, and the Black Country.

# REAL LABOUR

# THE BIOGRAPHY OF DENNIS TURNER

## Contents

# Preface

Dennis Turner became involved in his first industrial dispute as a choir boy at the age of 12, joined the Labour Party at 17, and went on to lead an eventful political life as a steel workers' leader, co-operator, MP, and member of the Lords.

In his later years as Lord Bilston, a Labour working peer, he might often be found supping his favourite pint in the Strangers' Bar among his parliamentary colleagues and friends. Always smartly turned out in a grey suit matching his mop of strikingly-grey hair, he stood 5 feet 8 inches in height and was stockily built. His disarming grin and twinkling blue eyes, set deep in a rugged but attractive face, made him instantly recognisable. Everyone who met him could sense immediately his sympathy for the human condition, his determination to help wherever he could, his always amiable exercise of authority, and his unshakeable firmness of social purpose. Woe betide those who would harm the just cause of his people!

Dennis Turner was born in 1942 in Bradley, the Black Country village renowned as the site where John Wilkinson, the ironmaster, invented a machine capable of boring the cylinders for Boulton and Watt's steam engines.

Like his father before him, Dennis worked nearby at the Bilston steel works, and was a member of the Iron and Steel Trades Confederation (ISTC) trade union. After the closure of the steel works, he joined with other redundant colleagues to set up the Springvale Co-operative.

In 1966, when he was 23, he was elected to Wolverhampton Borough Council as its youngest-ever councillor. Twenty-one years later, in the general election of 1987, he became the member of parliament for Wolverhampton South East constituency, taking the place of his political mentor and friend, the oldest sitting member of the House, Bob Edwards. When the Labour Party, under

Tony Blair's leadership, came into power in 1997, Clare Short, the Secretary of State for International Development, chose Dennis as her parliamentary private secretary.

In 2005, Dennis Turner entered the House of Lords, assuming the title of Baron Bilston of Bilston in the County of West Midlands. He insisted that he sat there merely as a working peer to serve the political interests of his party, and had no interest whatsoever in the trappings of office, a claim born out locally on his Black Country home territory, where anyone addressing him as 'Lord' was corrected and told to call him 'Dennis'. He joked to friends that if they found 'Dennis' over-familiar, then to stick to 'Comrade'.

At local level, Dennis Turner achieved in later life the unsurpassed status of a much-loved Labour Party and Black Country icon. The reputation had been earned through his ceaseless campaigning for local causes, his contribution to the development of a wide range of social services, his close attention to casework and the welfare of his constituents, and his self-evident affection for the people, the places, the pastimes and the pleasures of his Black Country home town.

His first major political challenge, taken on at the age of 31, was to chair the joint union action committee set up to convince the government and the British Steel Corporation that the Bilston steel works was a profitable plant and should not be shut down. Jobs throughout the Black Country depended on its steel. At one stage, to prevent the creeping closure of the plant and maintain its profitability, the workers assumed control of the works and re-bricked and re-fired a blast furnace which the management had taken out of service.

The steel workers' take-over of production at Bilston, under Dennis's leadership, was on a par with the 'work-in' led by Jimmy Reid to save shipbuilding on the Upper Clyde, but has remained largely unsung except in Bilston itself.

Even after the Bilston steel works were closed, Dennis continued the struggle to save the steel industry. He was selected to chair the Iron and Steel Trades Confederation's strike co-ordination committee, playing his part on the picket line alongside his brother, Bert, during the bitter steel strike of Spring 1980.

When the Bilston steel works eventually closed, the working-class communities, which had grown up around it, were not abandoned. Dennis, with nine other redundant workers, rented the works social facilities, and set up the Springvale Sports and Social Club as a workers' cooperative. Their purpose was to provide a meeting place, with an extensive range of social activities, for every individual, group, club, or association, in the south-east of Wolverhampton.

Dennis also served as a councillor on Wolverhampton Council for 20 years, from 1966 to 1986. During this time, he always represented the seat of Bilston East, which covered the district of Bradley in which he was born. He stood down in 1986, only to contest the Wolverhampton South East constituency, which had at its centre his home town – the former Black Country Borough of Bilston.

Dennis served on the council in different capacities, chairing a variety of committees and becoming deputy Labour council leader. He used his offices unsparingly to develop and improve local services for Wolverhampton people, taking a special interest in the vulnerable, the elderly, children, the young unemployed, victims of domestic violence, and minority groups. Recognising early on the importance of sustaining and attracting investment to the town, he first gave strategic direction to the council's Economic Development Committee. As employment rose in the early 1980s to unprecedented post-war heights, he made sure the council played a full part in alleviating unemployment and providing innovative high-quality youth training schemes.

In his capacity as chair of the post-Seebohm Social Services Committee, he secured the funds to build or refurbish a large number of municipally-run residential homes for the elderly and facilities for young people. He took a particular interest in establishing a hostel for single homeless men, a women's refuge, and specialist facilities for the town's ethnic minorities. Through the Housing Committee, he presided over the implementation of an extensive council house building programme and a plan to decentralise the stock to local housing offices on estates across the town, aimed at making the housing department more accountable to tenants.

As a member of the Education Committee, he was a strong advocate of its policy of establishing new purpose-built comprehensive schools throughout the borough. As chair of the Further Education Sub-Committee, he was responsible for developing and driving through an open-access tertiary education policy, which resulted in the creation of the radical Bilston Community College, which significantly extended further and adult educational facilities in the south-east of the borough to reach those parts of the population that traditional education had hitherto failed to reach.

John Bird, the Labour leader of the council, recognising Dennis's cultural interests, put him in charge of reopening Wolverhampton's insolvent Grand Theatre, a job he took on with a characteristic creative vigour. Dennis not only managed to tap into new sources of funding, but to engage in an innovative anti-elitist strategy of 'people's theatre', involving community groups, school drama classes, troupes of radical actors, and a diversified programme of pantomimes, musicals, and shows, many staged by local amateur dramatic societies.

Standing as a Co-operative Party candidate for Wolverhampton South East, Dennis was elected to parliament in 1987 with a majority of 6,395 over his Conservative rival, increasing that figure to 10,240 in 1992, and 15,182 in 1997, when he polled 63.7 per cent of votes cast. On first entering the House, he occupied a seat on the opposition back benches for ten long years, until the Labour general election victory of 1997. In this time, he served as the West Midlands and the education Labour whip, and helped form the All-Party

Parliamentary Group for Further Education, and the All-Party Parliamentary Group on Local Government.

When Labour eventually came to power, Dennis was made chair of the Catering Committee, which oversaw the Commons' catering and retail services, including the bar, restaurants and cafeteria. He used the position to good effect, to introduce Fairtrade goods, making the House of Commons the first major British public institution to do so. Having arranged for parties of senior citizens from his constituency to visit Westminster, Dennis was aware of the limited facilities in parliament for providing hospitality for larger groups. The Commons Jubilee Café was created to accommodate just such visitors.

As Clare Short's parliamentary private secretary, Dennis assisted with the planning and bringing into being of the new Department for International Development (DfID), and the adoption of the radical 'millennium development goals', which put a stop to the use of overseas aid to promote chauvinistic short-term commercial interests.

Dennis was probably best known for his persistent campaign for a fair pint of ale – to amend Weights and Measures legislation to guarantee a full liquid pint of beer. His private member's bill failed in the face of vested interests, but his efforts earned him a much-appreciated national award from the Campaign for Real Ale.

Throughout his parliamentary life, Dennis worked tirelessly for his beloved home town of Bilston, seeking to retain the memory of its iron and steel production to serve as a source of pride and inspiration for future generations. Today, Bilston High Street, market, and surrounding buildings and roads, are marked out from the rest of Wolverhampton by a set of monumental works of art and heavy steel street furniture, transforming the vicinity into a unique and impressive sculpture park.

In 2005, Dennis stood down as an MP, but was made a life peer, with the title of Baron Bilston of Bilston in the County of West Midlands. As a 'working peer', he continued to campaign ceaselessly for good causes, championing in particular the interests of the people of Wolverhampton and the Black Country, measures to reduce poverty, and the provision of further education and training to transform the economic prospects of individuals and their communities.

Over the more than 25 years that Dennis spent at Westminster, he earned the reputation of a hard-working affable loyal and characterful member of the Labour Party, much loved by colleagues on both sides of the House. Tony Blair described him as an "unspoken hero of the Labour Party", "loyal, unassuming, utterly committed to, and in touch with the people of Wolverhampton". Neil Kinnock saw him as epitomising all that was best about the Labour movement: "that special mixture of common sense and enlightenment, of feet on the ground and eyes on the horizon".

Pat McFadden, who took Dennis's seat when he was made a peer, commented on his unswerving loyalty to the Labour Party: "He was uncomfortable with some of New Labour policies, especially in regard to health and education, but he never went into opposition mode against his own government."

Dennis died on the 25th February 2014, surrounded by his family at home in Bradley, Bilston, in the heart of the Black Country. He was optimistic to the end about the power of individuals within their communities to transform their lives. He was fond of quoting the words of William Morris: "The Cause alone is worthy till the good days bring the best". The day would come, he earnestly believed, "when all our citizens are more equal, and more equally share in the wealth that they have helped to create. That day, we shall celebrate society's triumph over poverty and despair" (Lords Hansard, Lord Bilston, 8 May 2008, Column 735).

Dennis leaves his wife Pat, his two children, Brendon and Jenny, granddaughter, Bella, and his beloved older brother, Bert.

# Chapter 1

## Chasing the rag-and-bone man

## Dennis's birth

Dennis was born on the 26th August 1942 in Lord Street, Bradley (pronounced 'Braidley'), at that time part of the Borough of Bilston.[1] His father was Thomas Herbert (Bert) Turner, a steel worker, and his mother, Mary Elizabeth (Molly) Turner, née Peasley. Dennis was Bert and Molly's third child. His sister, Beryl, had been born in 1935, and brother, Thomas Herbert (named after his father, and like him known to everyone as 'Bert') in 1937. Dennis shared his first name with Dennis Hickman, the son of Fred Hickman, roll maker, and best friend of his father, Thomas.[2]

## Dennis's parents

Dennis's father, Bert, was born in Lane Head, Willenhall, and was living in lodgings in Bilston when he met his future wife, Molly. Molly's family lived near the Fiery Holes, once the site of a foundry established by John Wilkinson, the renowned ironmaster. She was one of the five children of Ben Peasley, a boatman or bargeman, who transported cargoes of coal, sand, gravel and stone by narrow boat along the canal network.[3]

Bert Turner's father had owned ten horses and carts which were used to take scrap metal to the steel works, but Bert was only 12 years old when he died, leaving the family in dire straits. The haulage business passed to an uncle.[4]

Bert went to work in the rolling mill at the Bilston steel works. When Dennis was born, Bert had a job there as one of a team of six men, armed with tongs, who carried the glowing ingots from the 14-inch mill, through a series of passes, to reduce the width of the bar. The heat in the works was so intense that the workmen had to drink barley water continually to prevent dehydration.[5]

As a steel worker during the second world war, Bert was in a reserved occupation, but insisted on volunteering to fight, and was sent to Catterick, where he joined the REME ( Royal Electrical and Mechanical Engineers) to serve in France and Germany.[6]

The heavy work in the rolling mill affected Bert's health. After bouts of absence due to sickness, including two due to pneumonia, he was found a less onerous job with the plant's gas turbines. Bert died in 1981 at the age of 71, Molly in 1974 when she was only 64, both having led very arduous lives.[7]

## Scarlet fever

When he was eight years old, Dennis developed scarlet fever which, before the availability of antibiotics, was a major cause of child mortality. With its characteristic symptoms of red rash, sore throat and fever, it was caught from inhalation, and children diagnosed with the disease were put into quarantine. Dennis, who nearly died, was confined to Moxley Sanatorium for six weeks. He remembered that he was not allowed to have visitors, and his mother could only speak to him through a glass partition. He found this a lonely and frightening experience and was much relieved to be restored to the company of the crowded family home.[8]  He speculated that this childhood affliction may have been the source of his respiratory problems in later life.[9]

Despite the poverty in which he lived as a child, Dennis described his home as "a place with love in it".[10]

## The back-to-back house where Dennis was born

The house where Dennis was born and brought up for the first seven years of his life was a typical Victorian back-to-back, with one room on the ground floor and two upstairs, a coal cellar, and a communal brew house, water tap, and lavatory in the yard. The downstairs living room had a coal-burning black-leaded grate, hob and spit, which were used for cooking. Light was provided at night from a gas mantle.[11]

When Dennis was born, Aunt Kate, Molly's sister, came to stay to look after mother and child, all five family members – Molly, Kate, Beryl, Bert (Junior), and baby Dennis – finding space to sleep in the two upstairs rooms. The family was desperately poor, a situation made worse by Bert Senior's periods of illness, when the family had to survive on a benefit of 7s 6d a week, the recollection of which always reduced Dennis to tears.[12]

## Day-old chicks

The Turner family had an allotment and, in his spare time, old Bert Turner kept poultry and turkeys which supplemented the family's diet and income and fed many of the residents of Lord Street at Christmas time. Len Bradbury, Dennis's childhood friend, recalled how he and Dennis once sold Bert's war-time greatcoat for a pittance to a rag-and-bone man. The boys then used the money to buy some fluffy day-old chicks which appealed to them.

When Dennis's mother, Molly, discovered what the boys had done, she was forced to chase around Bradley in pursuit of the rag-and-bone man in order to recover the vital old coat, which had to double in winter as a blanket on one of the beds.[13]

Of the 22 day-old chicks, 21 were kept warm under the hob, but one was given to Len who, on reaching home, placed it for safety on the kitchen table. Unfortunately, the family dog sprang up and bit the head off his new pet. Dennis regretted to the last his childhood selfishness in never thinking to offer Len a replacement bird.[14]

Dennis and Len used to go to the children's matinée 'flicks' at the Odeon. They reminisced about the day that the cinema staged a pet competition. Dennis entered his father's canary in its cage, while Len took along his pet mouse. To Dennis's surprise, the mouse won first prize, and the superior Turner canary came second. When the boys returned to Dennis's house, the mouse escaped, managing to run up the wall behind the wallpaper, making a channel as it went, before it was recaptured. The story was told to illustrate the physical dampness and chill prevailing in the Turners' home.[15,16]

## The council house in Lord Street West

In 1949, the Turner family moved from the back-to-back house in Lord Street, Bradley, to a council house close by, at 6 Powell Place, off Lord Street West. As one of the first council houses to be built soon after the first world war, the property had far more space: three bedrooms, a parlour with hob, and a scullery, but it was still lit entirely by gas.[17]

## School

At the age of 5, Dennis was sent to St Martin's Church of England School in Slater Street, the only primary school in Bradley, administered by Staffordshire County Council. While entitled to a ration of the recently-introduced free school milk, Dennis disliked the stuff intensely and gave his third of a pint to the other children.[18]

As well as providing milk to children under 18, RAB Butler's Education Act of 1944 raised the school leaving age to 15 and brought in state-funded secondary school education for all. But it also resulted in a tripartite system of secondary grammar, technical and modern schools, and a competitive examination at the age of eleven – known as the eleven plus – to select pupils for the highly-prized grammar school places. Unsurprisingly, along with the vast majority of children from poor working-class backgrounds, Dennis failed the eleven plus and was sent with others from Bradley to Stonefield Secondary Modern School on Prosser Street in Bilston.[19] Len Bradbury recalled that Dennis was a year ahead of him at school, and in the A stream, always smart, curious, inquiring, and in command of the latest playground project.[20]

## The Monkey's Paw

Dennis's favourite subject was English and, from an early age, he showed a fondness for drama and poetry. Dennis recalled, in particular, the part he played as Mrs White - the mother – in the school play: 'The Monkey's Paw', produced by Ron Harbridge, the school's talented drama teacher.[21] This was a horror story written by William Jacobs and made into a one-act melodrama in 1903.

It tells of a monkey's paw charm with mysterious powers to grant three wishes. Mr White is warned of the charm's dangers, but chooses to ignore them. He uses his first wish for £200 to pay off the debt on his family home. The Whites' son, Herbert, is then mangled to death by the machinery at his work place, and the family are given £200 in compensation.

With both parents stricken with grief, Mr White uses his second wish to bring his son back to life. The resurrected Herbert comes knocking at the door, but Mrs White (Dennis in long skirt, blouse and wig) struggles to keep it locked, knowing that as a result of his terrible accident, her son must be horribly deformed. She uses the third and final wish of the monkey's paw charm to cause the son to die, and return to the untroubled peace of the grave.

The knocking stops and the door at last is opened, but no one is there. Dennis recalled the music reaching a crescendo and the shocked suspense of the audience.[22] Older Bradley residents still remember 'The Monkey's Paw' and the part Dennis played in the drama, which resonated with them, as the Black Country experienced more than its fair share of factory and mining accidents.

Stonefield later became Hall Green School in the 1970s and Bilston High School in the 1980s. Dennis and Pat's two children, Brendon and Jenny, were both sent to Bilston High School, the comprehensive school nearest to the Turners' home in Bradley. Bilston High School's buildings were subsequently taken over by Parkfield High School, which was itself replaced in 2009 by the South Wolverhampton and Bilston Academy. The academy moved into its £25 million new building in Dudley Street, Bilston, in 2012.

Dennis was keen to dispel the myth that a working person's education came to an end on leaving school, citing the essential self-education of the work place, pub and club. He stressed, in particular, the mental arithmetic and logical inference required when playing crib, dominoes and darts. Many working men's clubs, he pointed out, had quiet reading rooms and their own libraries, where members would study and write letters.[23]

## St Martin's church

Dennis and his friend, Len, were members of the nearby St Martin's church. The church has since been demolished, but the church hall and former school buildings are still visible from 'Aubyn', on King Street – the house where Dennis and wife, Pat, were resident when this biography was written. Dennis and Len recalled the various vicars – Reverends Jenkins, Dentith, Heighway, Fisher, Moseley, etc. – and the church activities they sponsored. Len explained that Bradley people lent towards either the Anglican Church or the Methodist/Wesleyan Chapels, whose respective congregations tended to be concentrated in certain streets in the neighbourhood. The Anglican St Martin's sponsored the Bradley Boys Scouts, and Dennis and Len were in its Bulldog Patrol. Children, whose parents were Methodists or Wesleyans, were more likely to be members of the Boys' Brigade.[24] (Appreciative of Dennis's vigorous and enduring commitment to their cause, the Wolverhampton East District Scouts placed a tribute in the *Express & Star* on his death, which read, to 'a true Scout and a great supporter'.[25])

The Reverend Dentith made a lasting impression on the youthful Dennis, inspiring him to become a devout Christian and life-long member of the Anglican Communion. Indeed, at the age of 17, Dennis seriously considered training to become a minister of religion, but discovered that he was able to satisfy his conviction and realise, what he termed, a 'practical Christianity' through the agency of the Labour Party, which he joined at roughly the same time that he felt his religious calling.[26] When asked about his favourite reading matter, Dennis mentioned two books in particular: *The New Testament*, and Robert Tressell's *The Ragged Trousered Philanthropists*.[27]

Dennis was anxious to point out that, although he personally happened to be a Christian, all religions – Hinduism, Islam, Judaism, Sikhism, etc. – had a positive contribution to make to the good of the community. His Christianity was a way of expressing his love of 'the good community', where people supported one another, and of establishing 'the New Jerusalem'. His guiding light, he said, was his intense love of the human beings that constituted his vision of community. His abiding belief was in how much we could all achieve if we pulled together for the common good. He had no interest whatsoever in whether people gave themselves a religious or non-religious label, believing that their true selves were instantly illuminated by the contribution they made to the good of mankind as a whole.[28] It was self-evident that Dennis's political convictions and drive arose directly from a mainstream Christian socialist tradition.

Despite his deep respect for Christian institutions, he was not a regular churchgoer, and did not seek solace in religion as his final illness progressed, preferring instead, in his last hours of consciousness, to watch the jump racing on television in the company of his son, who was sent out to place his bets.

**Dennis's first industrial dispute**

From a very young age, Dennis found himself in possession of a fine singing voice, which he made good use of throughout his life. As a member of St Martin's church choir, he was able to 'sell' his vocal powers, which resulted in his becoming involved in his first industrial dispute. The church choir found itself in great demand at the peak of the wedding season, which came towards the end of March, to enable newly-weds to claim back tax before the end of the tax year.

At that time of the year, there was a wedding every hour on a Saturday. Led by Dennis aged 11, whose idea it was, the choir boys approached the vicar, organist, and choir master, with the demand that the stipend that each was paid for singing at a wedding be doubled from one to two shillings. Their request was refused outright. (Dennis recalled that the vicar – the Reverend Heighway – was an intimidating burly Rugby-playing Welshman.)

In response, early on the Saturday morning, the choir boys staged a 'sit out' on the church steps, refusing to enter the church until their demand was met in full. Fearful of complaints from couples claiming that their big day had been ruined by the church's failure to deliver on its promises, the churchmen soon chose to meet the choir boys' demand, and thereafter they received 2s per wedding.[29] This anecdote reveals that, as with Dennis's socialism, the seeds of his trade unionism were, in all likelihood, first nurtured and brought to bloom within the Christian confines of the Anglican Church.

### First job at Thomas Perry

On leaving school at the age of 15, Dennis started work as an office boy at Thomas Perry, a steel roll maker, on Highfield Road, near the railway bridge in Bradley. The foundry had been built and equipped in 1926 with up-to-date facilities for roll making to meet the demands of newer high-speed rolling mills, wide-strip mills, and cold mills. It was modernised in 1940 to deal with the rolling of aluminium, copper and brass, and again in the mid 1960s. The factory would eventually close in 1980, at the same time as the neighbouring Bilston steel works – the steel works being its main domestic supplier.[30]

### Betterware salesman

Dennis stayed at Thomas Perry for two years before deciding at 17 to work as a freelance salesman for the Betterware Company. Betterware was founded in East London in 1928 and remains in business, marketing kitchenware and cleaning products through a country-wide network of self-employed distributors. As one of those distributors, Dennis worked for the next four years on the doorsteps of families in Bradley, Bilston, Coseley, and much of the rest of the Black Country. He recalled old Mrs Miles, the landlady of the Travellers Rest, down by the Fiery Holes on the Great Bridge Road, as being one of his best and most regular customers. She bought large quantities of lavender polish and took pride in putting a shine on the round wooden tables of her pub.[31]

He claims that the experience of selling mops, brushes and pans gave him a profound and lasting insight into the home lives of thousands of working-class people, whom he came to love and to understand. In hindsight, it seems obvious that it also honed his skills as an expert political canvasser and effective purveyor of the socialist ideal of a better society for working-class men and women.[32]

## Market trader

On giving up his job as a Betterware salesman, Dennis took a pitch on Bilston Market, where he sold what he called "fancy goods" – mostly menswear, womens' clothes and accessories, including socks and shoes. He told us that this had taught him the harsh economics of market life and the importance to the vendors of the council keeping the tolls for stalls as low as possible in order to retain competitive prices. With disdain, he still recalled how the Bilston market tolls were increased dramatically when Wolverhampton Council was put in charge![33]

When Dennis got a job at the steel works, he began to trade part time. He gave up his regular pitch altogether when he was elected to the council in 1966.[34] Nevertheless, he retained a life-long interest in market trading, as shown in his later positions as chair of the Local Government Association's Markets Committee and vice-chair of the All-Party Parliamentary Markets Group, and his role in amending the Pedlar's Act in the Lords in 2012.

# Chapter 2

## Youth mayor of Bilston

### Joining the Labour Party

The urban district of Bilston in South Staffordshire, which included that part of Bradley in which Dennis was brought up, was granted a Royal Charter to become a municipal borough in 1933. It was not until 1966 that the Borough of Bilston was abolished, and its territory divided, with most being incorporated into the Borough of Wolverhampton. At the same time, a parcel of Dennis's beloved Bradley was sliced away and given to the neighbouring Borough of Walsall. From the point of view of an older generation of Bilstonians, these were acts of political vandalism with consequences that they never found easy to forgive or forget.

In 1959, at the age of 17, Dennis joined the Bilston Constituency Labour Party, Bradley branch. The Bradley branch of the Labour Party met in the Swan Inn in Bradley, a stone's throw from Dennis's home. Asked why he joined the Labour Party at such a young age, Dennis mentioned his deep-felt conviction that action needed to be taken to improve the lot of the many Black Country families, like his own, who lived in debilitating poverty.[1] Bert, his father, though not a party member, was strongly committed to the Labour Party and its socialist programme, and particularly its aim of nationalising the steel industry.[2] Dennis was soon made chair of the Bilston Young Socialists.

Old Bert Turner had no time for whingers who stood on the sidelines complaining, and urged his sons to play an active part in community life. In 1958, he persuaded Bert Junior, aged 22, and Dennis, 16, to take on the jobs respectively of secretary and assistant secretary of the Bradley Ex-Servicemen's Social Club, chiding a somewhat reluctant Dennis with the taunt "your heart's too near your arse", a Black Country expression meaning, we were told, that "your commitment is undermined by your laziness or lack of action", or "you're really not pulling your weight". His father's comment stung Dennis ever afterwards into avoiding complacency and taking decisive personal action against injustice.[3]

## Benjamin Bilboe

The Bradley and Bilston into which Dennis was born had a history of left-wing radicalism. Everyone in Bradley knew of 'Poverty Bonk' (Bank), off Loxdale Street, which earned its name from the fact that it had been cleared by unemployed men paid a shilling a day on a government works scheme, when the unemployment rate in the local iron trade stood at 64 per cent.[4] The renowned Benjamin Bilboe (quite possibly the inspiration for JR Tolkien's Bilbo Baggins in *The Hobbit*) became leader of the Unemployed Workers' Movement which organised mass demonstrations at 'Poverty Bonk' in protest at the government scheme, which paid wages far below the trade union rate.[5]

Bilboe was arrested and charged with inciting a breach of the peace, but on refusing to be bound over, was sent to prison. During his detention, which only enhanced his popularity, he was returned as a councillor for the Bilston New Town Ward. Once elected to Bilston Council, he wasted no time in demanding action on unemployment, housing, and social services - coincidentally, what were to become the main concerns of the yet-to-be-born Dennis Turner.

The immensely popular Benjamin Bilboe successfully defended his council seat with large majorities and, in 1947, when Dennis was five years old, was made the mayor of Bilston. Born in 1902 in a caravan at Ironbridge, Shropshire, in 1900, Benjamin Bilboe, doyen of the local Labour Party, died in Bilston in 1951, as poor as he had lived[6], still much admired for his campaigns in the cause of those working in the metal industries, such as Bert Turner Senior.

**Frank Venton**

One of Dennis's oldest friends, much appreciated for his loyalty and life-time support, was Frank Venton. Like Dennis, Frank was born in Bradley and brought up in conditions of abject poverty. In 1928, when Frank was aged ten, he lost his mother from septicaemia, following the birth of his baby sister, Lily. His father developed tuberculosis and was taken to Prestwood Sanatorium, where he stayed for many months. Far from fit, his father chose to go home and search for work to support his impoverished family and, in desperation, was forced to take a job for 1s 6d a day, levelling ground at 'Poverty Bonk'. He died aged only 39, leaving Frank to fend for two young sisters.[7]

Frank described how he asked older relatives to vouch for him as he tried to persuade the local means-testing assistance board to help. The board took a long time to decide to pay the family a weekly allowance of 7s 6d for both of his sisters, but it gave no help with the weekly rent of 8s 4d which, once paid, left the three children with very little to live on. Frank Venton made the point of saying how thankful he was when the means test was finally abolished.[8]

Born in 1918, Frank served in the army in Europe during the Second World War and, afterwards, joined the Bradley branch of the Labour Party. In his youth, he had known Benjamin Bilboe, and was aged 33 when he died. Frank always helped Dennis in his election campaigns and, on occasions, served as his agent (when Dennis's brother, Bert, was unable to take on the role). In later life, Frank was best known for volunteering his services as the doorman at Springvale Sports and Social Club, where he would chat on Friday nights about the political events of the week.[9]

**The youth mayor**

Dennis demonstrated his youthful interest in campaigning and politics long before he was elected to Wolverhampton Borough Council. In the 1950s and 1960s, Staffordshire County Council had developed a network of vibrant youth clubs, aimed not only at entertaining young people, but at preparing them to participate as citizens in a democracy. The youth clubs in Bilston used to elect a youth mayor and mayoress, who were expected to represent the interests of the town's young people at civic gatherings and on other occasions. Dennis managed to persuade the young people to elect him as Bilston's youth mayor, a position he held for a year in 1960.[10]

## Bradley and District Senior Citizens' Centre

As might have been expected, one of Dennis's first contributions to Bilston and Wolverhampton was to involve himself in a vigorous community campaign on behalf of old-age pensioners. In the aftermath of the second world war, Bradley old-age pensioners had asked for a place to meet. With so little property available, the local council had given them the keys to the neighbourhood's abandoned decontamination centre. Here for a while, the old men and old women used to gather separately on different days of the week, the men led by 'Stumper' Tinsley, the women by his wife. The two groups used to quarrel incessantly over the days they were allocated at the centre and all the other issues related to the way it was run.[11]

Recognising the gross inadequacy of the existing provision, the Bilston Labour Party, under Dennis's direction, set up the Bradley Old-Age Pensioners' Working Party, which joined with the local churches, and brought everyone on board, to raise funds for the construction of a brand-new facility. In 1967, the working party, with Dennis as its chair, organised a Bradley gala, opened by Jack Bodell, the boxer, which managed to raise the sum of £1,000. This popular fund-raising event was continued year after year.[12]

After Bilston and Bradley became part of Wolverhampton in 1966, Dennis was approached by Mr T D Holloway, Wolverhampton's chief welfare officer, with the suggestion that the new centre incorporate a facility for providing 'meals on wheels'. This proposal was readily taken on board and the working party, after a sustained fund-raising campaign lasting nine years, and with extra assistance from the council, was able to commission a high-quality brick building, with a well-equipped kitchen.[13]

The commemorative plaque at the entrance to the Bradley Senior Citizens' Centre, at Coronation Park on Wilkinson Avenue, states that the building was officially opened on the 20th March 1971 by Councillor Dennis Turner on behalf of the Bradley Trust Committee. In 2013, after 42 years, Dennis was still secretary to the trustees of Bradley and District Senior Citizens' Centre. Throughout his life, he never ceased campaigning on behalf of older people. For example, in 1993, he raised a petition of nearly 3,000 signatures to defend the free bus travel concession for pensioners.

**Bilston steel works**

After his stint as a salesman and market trader, Dennis followed his father and his brother into the Bilston steel works. In 1963, he was taken on as a stocktaker at the finishing end of the steel-making process, checking the billets, rounds, slabs and blooms for despatch to local Black Country rolling and forging mills for re-rolling and reshaping.[14]

When he joined the works in 1963, it was still the privately-owned Stewarts and Lloyds Ltd – the company which had taken it over from Alfred Hickman Ltd in 1920. The site was dominated by the enormous 'Elisabeth' blast furnace, named after the daughter of the Stewarts and Lloyds company chair. Completed in 1954, 'Big Lizzy', as she was popularly known, produced 275,000 tons of steel a year, and was later estimated to have made 5.5 million tons over her lifetime.

In 1966, under the Labour Government of Harold Wilson, Stewarts and Lloyds was nationalised to form part of the British Steel Corporation. At around the same time, Dennis was promoted to become the works transport controller, despatching lorry-loads of steel to destinations in the Black Country and nation-wide, a post he retained until the closure of the works in 1980.[15] The customers, he affirmed, swore by the quality of British steel. In 1966, the workforce saw only a rosy future in the nationalisation of the plant and could not have envisaged that a future Labour government would be responsible for the decision to close the site, resulting in mass redundancy.

# Chapter 3

## Wolverhampton's youngest councillor

### Election to Wolverhampton Borough Council

Under the West Midlands Order 1965, made by the Minister of Housing and Local Government, and approved by parliament on the 16th December 1965, local government in the Black Country was extensively reorganised. On the 1st April 1966, the existing County Borough of Wolverhampton was enlarged to include most of Bilston, Wednesfield, and Tettenhall, a large part of Coseley, and small parts of Darlaston, Sedgley, Seisdon and Willenhall. The new single-tier arrangements were aimed at bringing council services closer to local populations, providing more adequate resources, increasing co-operation, and improving people's understanding of government structures.[1]

With such widespread changes to the borough boundaries, elections were held on the 17th March 1966 to fill seats for the 20 wards constituting the newly-formed Wolverhampton Borough Council.[2] Shortly afterwards, the *Express & Star* reported on the 'wave of sorrow' sweeping 'through the old council chambers' and swirling 'around the leather chairs and polished tables last night, as the smaller Black Country councils met for the last time'.[3]

It was in this nostalgic atmosphere that Dennis, aged only 23, was elected, with a majority of 500 votes, as the youngest-ever Wolverhampton councillor for the ward of Bilston East (which included most of Bradley).[4] (Many years later, when they sat together on Wolverhampton Council, Dennis and Mel Chevannes agreed that they had both broken council records, he being the youngest councillor, and she the first-ever black Caribbean to be elected. Drawing on the sly logic of a Black Country Enoch and Eli joke, Dennis was quick to point out to her: "You'll always be Wolverhampton's first black councillor, but I'm only the youngest till they go and elect a 22-year-old!")

Dennis continued to contest and hold the same seat of Bilston East for the duration of his unbroken 20 years on the council, only stepping down in 1986 to prepare for his 1987 general election fight. In all the local elections he fought, he was always returned with a handsome majority – in 1973, 1978 and 1982, of well over a thousand votes.

## Dennis's socialism

Well before he became a councillor, Dennis had arrived at a remarkably sophisticated concept of socialism, based on municipal enterprise and local co-operation. It derived from the success of a city, such as Birmingham, in providing its own municipally-run sewage system, water, gas, and electricity supply, trams and buses, and banking structure. Bilston and Wolverhampton, too, had had their own water pumping stations, gas works, electricity supply, and house-building projects.[5]

Dennis saw no reason why democratically-controlled municipal enterprise could not be extended further to compete with the private sector. In his view, this would be to everyone's benefit. He had in mind a fourfold approach to economic development and progress, involving major nationalised industries (such as the railways, and coal and steel production), municipal enterprises (to deliver water, public transport, houses, schools and welfare services), and co-operative businesses (to provide goods such as groceries, household furniture, domestic equipment and other services), with the private sector left to supply what was left – essentially the non-essentials to life.[6]

He was to join Wolverhampton Borough Council with this mindset and, almost half a century later, wished us to place on record that he had not changed his opinion one jot on his preferred arrangements for the relations of production, distribution and exchange.[7] He was frustrated, nevertheless, in the realisation that he had been unable to persuade Labour members, fellow councillors, colleagues in parliament – or Tony Blair himself – of the merits of his own preferred eclectic form of the socialist economy. And he thought it entirely unacceptable that, especially on a Labour watch, council enterprises and services had been privatised.[8]

To his mind, one of the most regrettable examples of the adverse consequences of the failure to promote local authority service provision had been the transfer of residential homes for old people to private care providers in pursuit of profit, with the predictable abuses exemplified by the scandal of Southern Cross.[9]

## On joining the council

When Dennis joined the council, he found himself viewed as a left-wing extremist, particularly in regard to his ambitious plans for extending the local municipal economy. At odds with some of his more elderly Labour colleagues, and watched closely by a wary Dennis Birch, the leader of the Labour Group,[10] the articulate young councillor was allocated, nevertheless, to the Transport Committee which was responsible for running Wolverhampton's buses. He was made its spokesman, but found it difficult to accept, or publicly defend, the Transport Committee's decision to refuse its bus drivers and conductors the right to wear turbans and beards while on duty.[11]

## Campaign to save the old Bilston Market Hall

As a councillor for Bilston East, Dennis was at the centre of a local campaign to save Bilston's magnificent brick-built market hall, with its four long aisles lined with a multiplicity of stalls. Such was its popularity as the biggest and best market in the region – the Black Country Mecca of its day - that on Fridays and Saturdays, thousands would descend on it by bus, car and foot, looking for bargains.

By 1967, despite its popularity, the market was showing signs of age. It no longer complied with new hygiene regulations and the Wolverhampton borough engineer claimed that its metal roof beams were badly corroded, resulting in serious structural defects.[12] Wolverhampton Council Markets Committee, which had recently assumed responsibility for the building, was urged by the officers to order the demolition of the hall and to have a new one built.

As a former stall holder, Dennis, who loved the business and bustle of the place, was determined to prevent this happening, arguing instead for a modernisation programme – to include the installation of new taps and glass partitions to deal with the hygiene issues – which, in his view, would preserve the best of the old and cost the council far less.

The campaign was hotly fought but, with the loss of the council to the Conservatives, Bob Campbell (the Conservative chair of the Markets Committee, and a councillor for Bilston North), forced through the decision to demolish and rebuild a new, but far less imposing edifice.[13]

**Bilston institutions under threat**

Other cherished institutions of Bilston were also threatened by their incorporation into Wolverhampton. The historic Bilston Town Hall, whose foundation stone had been laid on the 2nd April 1872, was declared structurally unsound, and the activities held on its premises - such as the popular tea dances – were brought to an end. The Bilston Museum and Art Gallery's trades and crafts display was closed and its exhibits dispersed elsewhere. While opposition at the time proved futile, this failure to respect the town's proud legacy remained a bitter Bilston folk memory. The story of how Dennis, some thirty years later, went about addressing that affront is told in Chapter 13.

**The 'immorality rule'**

In the early 1970s, the council declined to find suitable alternative accommodation for one of Dennis's Bradley constituents who had broken up with his wife. Ted Lane, a senior Labour politician, was a staunch Catholic, opposed to divorce, and a defender of the council's so-called 'immorality rule', introduced to discourage marital separation or divorce. If a man left the family home under these circumstances, the only accommodation the council could suggest was a hostel.

Regarding the policy as heartless, Dennis toured the public houses of Bilston, explaining the consequences of the council's policy and gathering signatures for a petition calling for a change to the rule.[14] This popular pressure forced the Housing Committee to change its policy and Dennis's constituent was eventually re-housed.

## The Civic Catering Committee

As mentioned above, Dennis was very much in favour of developing civic enterprise and the economic self-sufficiency of the council which, he believed, was perfectly capable of competing on an even playing field with the private sector. The council owned its own farm and ran a number of restaurants and cafés, not only for its own employees but for the general public, who could eat there or hire the catering facilities for public functions, such as weddings.

Under Labour control, the council had gone on running a successful and profitable municipal catering business, but when the Conservatives came to power between 1967 and 1971, they began to challenge this taken-for-granted approach to the delivery of local services and roll back the practice of municipal socialism.

Dennis, as a member of the Civic Catering Committee, was infuriated by the Conservative decision to close down the outlets around the town, in particular the 'Woolpack' a stylish modern restaurant in Wolverhampton's recently-constructed market block.[15] His friend and colleague, Councillor Ian Claymore, recalls how Dennis marched into the committee room and presented Patrick Lacey, the Conservative chair of the committee, with a large wreath marked, 'RIP Municipal Catering', to applause from Labour members and excitement from the press. The wreath remained on the committee room table for the duration of the meeting while the decision to divest was taken.[16]

## The Economic Development Committee

When Labour regained control in 1972, Dennis became chair of the Economic Development Committee and, later, deputy leader of the council's Labour Group. As chair of the Economic Development Committee, Dennis explored the limits of the council's powers to support local industry in order to save the jobs of Wolverhampton workers.[17] Some of the proposals emanating from the committee caused the town clerk, Kenneth Williams, to intervene and urge the Labour leader to rein in his eager young councillor.

Dennis involved himself in the campaign to save the celebrated Norton Villiers motorbikes, which were still being built in Wolverhampton in the early 1970s. Together with his friend and fellow councillor, Ken Purchase, who was chair of the Finance Committee, Dennis sought to mount a municipal project funded by the product of a 3d rate to help the workers form a co-operative to take over the ailing company.[18] Dennis and Ken travelled up and down the country in support of the company but, despite wide support in the Labour Group, the leader felt obliged to call a halt to the local authority's involvement.

On another occasion, the unions at the Bilston Bath Company (which became Bilston Allied Iron Founders) in Highfields Road, brought to Dennis's attention the company's cash-flow problems and the imminent threat of closure with attendant job loss. The company had 1,000 high-quality enamel iron baths in stock which, if a buyer could be found, might tide the company over by restoring it to credit. Thinking laterally, the Economic Development Committee came up with the idea that the baths might be purchased en masse by the council for installation in the new properties being constructed as part of the council's house building programme.[19] Dennis did not, in the end, persuade the council to agree to the arrangement.

Another of Dennis's schemes related closely to the council house refurbishment programme. He tried to prevail upon his fellow councillors to agree to open a municipal wallpaper and papering shop to sell a range of wallpapers and accessories to council house tenants, but could not even persuade Ken Purchase to support him.[20]

## A practical approach to racism and discrimination

Shortly after he was elected to the council, Dennis was confronted with an unsavoury incident of racial hostility in his Bradley ward. After spending a long time on the council house waiting list, the Buchanans – a black man and wife and their two children – had at last been offered a council maisonette.[21] White neighbours on either side had phoned the Wolverhampton *Express & Star*, and threatened to take a knife to Mr Buchanan, should he move into the property. Appalled by this behaviour, Dennis decided to call round to talk to his two constituents, using his personal charm and authority as their councillor to reason with them.[22]

"Alice what's this all about?"
"If he moves in, we'll stick a knife in him"
"How can you say a thing like that before you've even met the man? I think you owe him an apology."

Dennis persuaded both women to agree to a meeting at which they would apologise, and took along the amiable Mr Buchanan for an introduction. Within a week, the two women had contacted the *Express & Star* once more, this time with the news that they were organising a house-warming party to welcome the new tenants.[23]

Personal intervention, affable but firm persuasion, and intensely practical problem-solving were typical of Dennis's politics across the board, but especially in regard to matters of colour and race relations. In Wolverhampton, attitudes towards racial minorities were about to deteriorate disastrously as a result of what came to be described as Enoch Powell's 'political earthquake'.

## Enoch Powell's 'political earthquake'

Enoch Powell was the Conservative MP for Wolverhampton South West from 1950 to 1974. He was to make his infamous 'river-of-blood' speech on the 20 April 1968 to Conservatives in Birmingham.[24]
In emotive and inflammatory terms, he called for an end to the right of settlement for Commonwealth immigrants' dependents, measures to encourage 're-emigration' and total opposition to anti-discrimination legislation. Powell talked of a conversation he had had with a white constituent: "a middle-aged quite ordinary working man" employed in "one of our nationalised industries", who had told him of his desire to emigrate with his family overseas because in Britain "in fifteen or twenty years' time", the black man would "have the whip hand over the white man."

Whole areas, towns and parts of towns would soon be "occupied" by the immigrant population, and action had to be taken to prevent these "evils". Allowing the dependents of immigrants to join their families in Britain was like "watching a nation busily engaged in heaping up its own funeral pyre".

By way of illustration, he cited the example of an old lady in Wolverhampton who was now the only white woman in the street. She had had her windows broken, excreta pushed through her letter box, and had been verbally abused. When she went to the shops, she was followed by "charming wide-grinning piccaninnies", who called her "a racialist".

Edward Heath reacted to the speech by calling it "racialist in tone", and dismissing Enoch Powell from the shadow cabinet. Powell's 'river-of-blood' speech and his sacking from the Conservative frontbench generated intense excitement in Wolverhampton. Many Wulfrunians saw "our Enoch" as they called him, speaking for the town as a whole, and were proud of their association with him, and the expertise that they, as local residents, had now acquired in the field of race relations.

For many weeks, the prevailing topic of conversation consisted of complaints about immigrants and what to do about them: "they smell, they're violent, they take our jobs, they take our houses, they breed like rabbits, they live off the country, they cause disease, they don't want to mix", etc.[25]

## Workers' support for Enoch Powell

The national press highlighted the 1,500 dockers, chanting "We want Enoch", who marched from the West India Dock to parliament. Less well reported was the industrial action taken on Powell's behalf in Wolverhampton, Powell's political heartland. For example, one thousand of the 1,200 employees at Joseph Sankey GKN Works in Bradley, on Dennis's home territory, signed a petition in favour of Powell. One thousand workers at Norton Villiers, Wolverhampton, finished work half an hour early as a gesture of their support. Workers at Wolverhampton and Dudley Brewery stopped work for half a day to march to the town hall in order to hand in a petition protesting to the mayor about Powell's dismissal.[26]

## Support for Powell at the steel works

Dennis and his brother, Bert, along with other progressive trade unionists and shop stewards at the steel works, found themselves in an embattled minority, having to argue vehemently with fellow trade unionists and shop-floor workers, expressing overtly anti-immigrant and racist sentiments. Enoch Powell's speech not only made working-class racism commonplace and respectable, but blurred traditional class loyalties, resulting in a much bolder and broader challenge to the left-leaning, normally Labour-supporting, leadership. The shop stewards also had to deal with a marked increase of racial abuse, victimisation and violence on the shop floor, particularly when work forces were divided along racial lines.[27]

## Making a stand

Labour MPs, prominent Labour councillors, and members of the local Labour Party, were forced into making a stand. Such was the extremity of the situation on the ground that it was simply no longer possible to stay on the political sidelines.

Renee Short, Labour MP for Wolverhampton North East, pointed out that Powell was against everything working people had ever fought for and that it was simply crazy for them to march in his favour. Bob Edwards, Labour MP for Bilston, and general secretary of the Chemical Workers' Union, denounced the outbreak of pro-Powell strikes as against the spirit of international brotherhood on which the trade union movement was founded. Powell, in his view, had "stirred up race hatred in his aim to get the leadership of the Tory Party. It was purely a personal thing". Councillor John Bird, who was also secretary of the Wolverhampton North East Constituency Labour Party, hoped the speech would put an end to Powell's political career.

As a councillor and employee at the steel works, Dennis found himself having to argue vigorously with fellow workers and voters on the issue of the day by appealing to the importance of international solidarity and brotherhood, irrespective of colour, race, or national origin – values that he honed and campaigned for throughout his life. Dennis's logic was simple. The Asians and West Indians were fellow workers, selling their labour power and being exploited along with the rest. They should not be excluded from the class struggle, but signed up to the union with immediate effect to ensure they were paid the same rate as other employees. Nevertheless, getting this message across had been a pretty futile exercise at the time, with few prepared to listen.[28]

## Tackling racialism

By 1968, at least 20 per cent of the workforce at the steel works was of minority ethnic origin, many of them Indian. Dennis spoke of how he used to stand on a table in the works canteen in the amenity block every morning addressing the steel workers.

"I kept telling them that Enoch Powell didn't speak for us all and that union solidarity was the best way of fighting racialism. I got them to sign up en masse for the ISTC. Years later, when I stood for parliament, and I was out canvassing in Ettingshall, they would come to the door and say: 'I know you. You used to stand on the table in the canteen'."[29]

Since those early days, Dennis worked hard to eradicate Enoch Powell's divisive legacy by ensuring that all residents of Wolverhampton were treated equally and with the respect they deserved as human beings. In the process, he befriended and helped, directly or indirectly, and without favour, thousands of individuals from all of the city's communities. As with most other Labour councillors in office at the time, and for many years afterwards, he recognised and regretted the lasting damage done to Wolverhampton's reputation and image by the 'river-of-blood' speech.

Most of the town's major employers, including the council, colleges, schools, and the aerospace industry, found it immensely difficult thereafter to recruit staff from elsewhere in the country. Families were reluctant to relocate to a place with such allegedly troubled community relations.

**Young Volunteer Force Foundation**

In 1968/69, Dennis managed to secure council backing for the Young Volunteer Force Foundation, started by Anthony Steen in 1968. The YVFF set up its Wolverhampton office on the Dudley Road and began to involve young people in various innovative projects.[30] The council commissioned the YVFF to undertake a survey of Wolverhampton's rough sleepers and, with the help of sociology students from Bilston College of Further Education, a report was produced on the number of single homeless men sleeping in derelict properties in the town. As part of this exercise, Frank Reeves remembers accompanying Dennis on a visit to view the punitive

## Chair of the Social Services Committee

From the 12th June 1972, after Labour won control of the council, to 1979, when they lost it, Dennis was chair of the council's Social Services Committee. (He also served as deputy Labour leader from 1978 to 1986.) His stewardship of the Social Services Department came soon after measures were taken to implement the Seebohm Report of 1968. The report recommended integrating councils' children's, elderly and mental welfare departments into a single social services department aimed at co-ordinating services and reducing costs.

Dennis saw the re-organisation as an opportunity to improve and expand the town's welfare services.[2] He was aided in this enterprise by Councillor Ken Purchase, who, in the early 1970s, was chair of the Finance Committee, thus facilitating the transfer of funds to spend on the social services.[3] During this period, council provision for children and the elderly was overhauled in its entirety and accommodated in new purpose-built premises throughout the town. Dennis oversaw the construction or refurbishment of fourteen old people's homes and day centres.[4] For instance, Renée Short, the MP for Wolverhampton North East, was invited to open The Maltings, an extensive all-purpose day centre, on the 21st October 1977.[5]

In the 1980s, two-thirds of residential care home places nationally were provided by local authorities, and in Wolverhampton the proportion was considerably greater. By the mid-1990s, Wolverhampton Council embarked on plans to close or transfer its care homes to the private sector. By the new millennium, two-thirds of places were provided by the private sector, a trend that continues to grow. Both Dennis and Cllr Mel Chevannes, Dennis's successor as chair of Social Services in the 1980s, resisted the privatisation of care, regarding it as a profound and expensive mistake, injurious to the interests of old people as a whole.

In his time as chair, Dennis extended the range and scope of the town's social services, paying particular attention to facilities for adults and children with learning difficulties and the rehabilitation of people with mental illness.[6] In regard to the latter, Keith Elder, an officer of Mind, was co-opted to the committee to advise.[7] Public awareness was increasing of the dangers of patient institutionalisation, encouraged by the reading of Goffman's *Asylums* (1961), and the popularity of the film, *One Flew Over the Cuckoo's Nest* (1975).

The imperative was to close down the large mental hospitals and to disperse and rehabilitate people with a mental illness in the community. The principle of care in the community was widely accepted. In practice, however, it required small groups of patients to be accommodated in hostels throughout the town. Dispersal of this kind was frequently resisted. On hearing that a house close to them was to be allocated for the use of people with mental health issues, less enlightened residents would band together to oppose the plan, citing a possible risk to the safety of their families.

After one vociferous campaign to see off a hostel in the Bilston area, Dennis quietly arranged for Church House, a building in King Street in Bradley, next door to his own home, 'Ambleside', to be used instead. This serves as a telling example of his belief in the power of 'do as I do', in contrast to 'do as I say'.[8]

He took a special interest in the plight of single homeless men and the need to establish suitable hostel accommodation for them at a central location in the town, an initiative which eventually led to the construction of purpose-built premises on Thornley Street.[9] The Young Volunteers were also given a grant to open a soup kitchen at St George's House.[10]

In the face of intense Conservative opposition, Dennis secured funding for a hostel, sponsored by Wolverhampton Council for Community Relations, to accommodate young homeless black men.[11] A house on the Waterloo Road was also made available for the Afro-Caribbean Harambee Association, which provided similar facilities.[12] In the face of negative reporting in the local press and an evidently hostile political climate to providing any facility specifically targeted at meeting ethnic-minority needs, these were brave decisions.

Undeterred, Dennis persuaded Social Services Committee members to co-opt Aaron Haynes, the town's community relations officer, to enhance their understanding of the town's minority communities.[13] The committee minutes reveal that Dennis attended a seminar on the Race Relations bill in London on the 10th to the 12th September 1976.[14] In 1978, Dennis made sure the committee approved a decision to provide a day centre for elderly Asian men.[15]

## The Haven

Of all Dennis's achievements while chair of the Social Services Committee, the one he took most pride in was the decision to fund the Haven, a project providing hostels and help for homeless women, often the victims of domestic violence. At that time, very little help was provided for women who were assaulted and raped in the home, or found themselves made homeless as a consequence. Initially, Dennis made sure that the Haven was allocated various properties in different locations in the town, but he continued to press for further improvements in accommodation and security, which eventually led to the construction of a brand-new hostel.[16]

He also supported a separate refuge for Asian women, accepting fully the case for a culturally-sensitive targeted approach. This project received his energetic support, despite opposition at the time from Conservative councillors, who denounced it as 'discrimination in reverse', and from Asian leaders, who claimed it would undermine their close family ties and result in promiscuity and prostitution among their womenfolk.

Long after he left the Social Services Committee, Dennis continued promoting the Haven and local women's causes, providing a reference for the Haven's application in 2006 to the National Lottery for a grant to undertake work with the Ekaterina Crisis Centre – a women's project in Russia.[17]

Frequently dismissed by middle-class women party members, who had never met him personally, as an unreformed beer-swilling grey-hound-loving Black Country 'Andy Capp', Dennis was unswerving in his wholehearted commitment to women's rights. This he amply demonstrated by putting his back into the practical day-to-day struggles for equal pay, women's refuges and the victims of domestic violence (including specialist facilities for Asian women and girls), universal state-funded childcare provision, new nursery schools, hospital maternity wards, gynaecological units, and breast cancer charities.

**Saving the Grand Theatre**

Ever since his role in the Stonefield School play, 'The Monkey's Paw', Dennis had retained an interest in drama and the theatre. In his teenage years, he joined the Bilston Amateur Dramatic Society which met at Bilston Town Hall and staged productions of plays and musicals.[18] Given this early interest, it came as no surprise that Labour leader, Cllr John Bird, turned to Dennis to devise a plan to reopen Wolverhampton's insolvent Grand Theatre, which had closed its doors in the midst of the financial cuts of the early 1980s.[19]

Dennis realised immediately that the failed theatre not only needed a cash injection, but a whole new philosophy of providing drama and entertainment for all the people of Wolverhampton, to replace the former restricted repertoire of performances which appealed only to a minority cultural elite. The answer lay, as usual, in community action to save the theatre, and a strategy to extend the range of its audiences and shows.

The theatre was reopened and its programme diversified to include pantomime, musicals, and shows staged by amateur dramatic societies, not only from Wolverhampton, but from other parts of the Black Country and South Staffordshire. The new open-access policy was exemplified by the adaptation of the theatre to allow access for wheel-chair users and other disabled people, achieved with the help of a grant from the Social Services Committee – of which Dennis, of course, was chair.[20]

Dennis also encouraged and promoted troupes of local actors, such as those from the Zip and Gazebo theatres. He saw them as contributing not only to the popularity of the arts and acting, but to helping to solve the crisis of youth unemployment, through their work with schools, youth services, and youth training schemes. With this augmented role in mind, the council and other bodies in the town were able to provide grant aid from their various budgets to support Zip's community activities and other similar schemes.[21]

**Town clerk or chief executive?**

Related closely to Dennis's views on the promotion of municipal socialism and enterprise was his campaign to tackle compartmentalism. He convened a meeting at his house, 'Ambleside' in Bradley, of councillors and party members who he thought might be interested in improving the council's performance. He felt it was high time that the council worked as a co-operative entity, rather than as a set of separate departments, each delivering its own statutory minimal duties.[22]

He envisaged the council's work being divided into two corporate entities – a 'human' and a 'technical' interface – the 'human' providing a comprehensive portfolio of housing, social and educational services, the 'technical' dealing with, tendering, purchasing, building, refurbishment, and equipment.[23] Dennis felt his original proposals for a radical and thoroughgoing reorganisation along these lines foundered on the vested interests and insecurity of established officers and councillors alike.[24]

His ideas were to surface again when he was deputy council leader, with his proposal to replace the retiring town clerk with a chief executive. He saw this move as a means of transforming the council, conceived as a democratic legally-constituted body of separate departments, each with a limited set of powers, into a dynamic directed and unified organisation providing a wide range of services for the people of Wolverhampton. To this end, he had to persuade John Bird, the Labour leader, to take what was then the radical step of appointing a chief executive with economic and business credentials in place of a legally-orientated town clerk.[25]

The opportunity arose in 1985, with the retirement of Kenneth Williams, the Wolverhampton town clerk. In the face of opposition from more conservatively-inclined councillors, Dennis, together with fellow councillor, Ken Purchase, managed to appoint Michael Lyons, who had worked previously as deputy to Terry Pitt, the chief economic adviser to the West Midlands Metropolitan County Council. (Terry Pitt had previously advised Harold Wilson.)

The young Michael Lyons cut his teeth as chief executive of Wolverhampton Borough Council from 1985 to 1990, before moving to the same position at Nottingham County Council from 1990 to 1994, and Birmingham City Council from 1994 to 2001. He was knighted in January 2000 in recognition of his services to local government. In later life, Sir Michael's most celebrated role was as chair of the BBC Trust.

## Election to the West Midlands County Council

Following the Local Government Act 1972, elections were held in 1973 for the new West Midlands County Council, which was inaugurated a year later on 1 April 1974. Dennis piled up the votes in the two-ward Ettingshall and Springvale seat, winning with 3,921 votes, over the Conservative's 901, and the Communist's 181, a majority over his Tory rival of 3,020. That year, Labour won 73 of the county council's 104 seats.

Dennis was magnanimous in victory. Standing as his Communist opponent, Frank Reeves remembers him instructing the counting officer to give every disputed ballot "to Frank, cos he's going to need them".[26] This generosity towards a no-hoper, of course, was a way of ensuring the vote did not go to his Tory opponent. Forty years later, Frank is still able to boast that he is the only paid-up member of the Labour Party to have stood against Dennis in a council election.

With Labour in control on the West Midlands County Council from 1974 to 1977, Dennis was soon made vice chair of the county's Economic Development Committee, with Geoff Edge serving as chair, positions that were to prove useful in the struggle to keep open the Bilston steel works.

The West Midlands County Council existed for twelve years before it was abolished by Margaret Thatcher's government on 31 March 1986, along with the five other metropolitan county councils and the Greater London council. Its fossilised traces can still be seen in the fallow fourth year retained between the three successive years of elections for West Midlands metropolitan borough council seats.

# Chapter 5

## Seeing a man about a dog

### Black Country upbringing

Born and brought up in Bradley, Dennis and his older brother, Bert, were immersed in the male working-class culture of their place and time. They relished the intimacy, nurture and support of family, street and neighbourhood life; the Black Country dialect, accent, idiom and humour; and the traditional Black Country cookery, food, feasts and delicacies, such as faggots and mushy peas. They drank ale and beer brewed close by, at the Springfield, Banks's and Holden breweries or, more rudimentarily, in the brew houses still remaining at the rear of some of the traditional Black Country pubs, such as the Beacon in Sedgley.

Outside of the workplace, they participated in the popular local pastimes, sports, hobbies and amusements, becoming experts and enthusiasts in the process. They could have kept a pigeon loft and, at one point, Dennis did fly a pair of tumblers. But, from a young age, Dennis and Bert became enamoured of dogs and the working man's sport of grey-hound racing. Not surprisingly, many of the stories told about Dennis relate to his love of dogs, though none can accurately be termed 'shaggy-dog stories'.

### A dog's life

Bert Turner saw a beautiful blue greyhound at the Willenhall Stadium. After consulting with Dennis, the two brothers decided to buy the bitch for £5 – a great deal of money in those days – and to take her to Ray Wilkes, a private trainer at Wolverley to assess her potential. As Ray wound away, the animal chased through the grass after the hare, and Ray assured them that she made a good time. Subsequently, 'Torside Beauty', or 'Betty', as she was known, performed very well at a solo trial at Cradley Heath and it was decided to try her in a race with other dogs. This proved a disaster, as she showed no interest in the hare, but chased instead after the other greyhounds, attacking and biting them. Clearly, Betty was a fighter not a runner.[1]

Betty was taken home and kept at Bert's newly-acquired house at Bradley but, in the course of a couple of days, destroyed the interior, gnawing and scratching the doors and furniture. Soon afterwards, Bert and Dennis took Betty, together with Trigger, Dennis's other dog (a Labrador/German Shepherd cross), for a walk by the family allotment. Here, they encountered twenty lay-pullets. In front of the Turner family, Betty, aided and abetted by Trigger (to Dennis's eternal shame), ran at the chickens and, within the flash of eye, killed eight of them outright.[2]

Dennis and Bert's love of dogs and grey-hound racing, however, was not diminished in any way by the 'Torside Beauty' experience. From then on, however, all future greyhounds were kept in kennels and trained for the track by professionals.

When asked recently whether he still owned dogs, Dennis admitted that he and Bert currently kept five in kennels and raced them regularly at the Monmore Green Stadium.[3] His abiding interest in dogs was demonstrated by his chairmanship of the All-Party Parliamentary Greyhound Group, dedicated to raising parliamentary awareness of the issues relating to the greyhound industry and to promoting dog racing.[4]  With these aims undoubtedly in mind, he named one of his dogs, 'Division Belle'.

**The races**

Dennis and Bert were keen race goers, taking time out at various courses, such as Cheltenham, Chepstow (for the Welsh National), Ludlow, and Worcester.[5] Dennis had even travelled to Ireland to watch horse racing. He studied form and placed regular bets, but was canny, and rarely found himself out of pocket. Sometimes, when we turned up at his house, he would be watching the racing on television, but would turn away politely from the screen to greet us, unless the horse he had backed was about to win.

As might be expected, Dennis was libertarian in his attitude to gambling, believing that the restrictive laws of the past were largely based on a middle-class moral hypocrisy aimed at preventing working people from enjoying themselves.

## The Bert Williams connection

Dennis and Bert were part of a working-class community which divided the year into football and cricket seasons. With the exception of John Wilkinson, the 18th century ironmaster, Bradley's most famous son, without doubt, was Bert Williams – the 'Cat' – who signed for Wolverhampton Wanderers in 1945, making 420 appearances for the club as a goalkeeper, and helping his team win the FA Cup in 1949, and the League in 1953-54. He was called up in 1949 to play for England and earned 24 England caps.

Like Dennis, Bert Williams attended St Martin's Primary School. Bert started playing football for Bradley Methodist Church Boys' Brigade, but proved so outstanding that he was soon asked to play for the Walsall reserves. Bert Williams' dad was an acquaintance of Bert Turner Senior. Frank Venton, the Turner family's friend and a member of the Bilston Labour Party, used to play football with Bert Williams' brother, Walter.[6] On retiring from professional football, Bert ran a sports shop in Bilston and opened a gym there.

In recent years, the Turner brothers pressed for Bert Williams to be given the recognition he deserved on his home turf. On the 2nd February 1996, he was asked to open the Bilston Job Centre. Councillor Bert Turner persuaded Wolverhampton Council to call the new Bilston sports complex and swimming pool, the 'Bert Williams Leisure Centre'.[7] Bert, then in his 90s, was asked to open this magnificent facility. On the opening day, Saturday, 3rd December 2011, he claimed that to have the centre named after him was the greatest joy of his life. Bert lived in a residential home on Wolverhampton Street in Bilston until his death on the 19th January 2014 at New Cross Hospital.

## Council house repairs

Ken Purchase recounts that both his parents and Dennis's parents lived in council houses. Both he and Dennis were leading councillors and had, at different times, served as chairs of the council's Housing Committee. Ken pointed out, however, that for sound ethical and political reasons, neither he nor Dennis were prepared to take action on housing matters in regard to their own parents' housing conditions. He describes that on one occasion, when he was visiting the Turner family home at Powell Place, Bradley, Dennis's father, Bert, complained that his son might indeed be a councillor but that he wasn't prepared to lift a finger to help get the window frames fixed.[8]

## 'Ambleside'

Dennis went on living at home with his father, mother and Auntie Kate in Powell Place until 1973 when, he and MP, Bob Edwards, who had recently lost his wife, decided to club together to buy 'Ambleside', a spacious property in King Street nearby. It served as Bob's residence in the constituency, and a home and office for Dennis's campaigning and council work.[9]

## Political ambition

Soon after Dennis moved to 'Ambleside', he told his father that he had enjoyed the seven years he had spent on Wolverhampton Council and was considering standing for parliament.

Old Bert Turner later expressed his scepticism to his older son, Bert. Dennis could never be an MP, could he?

Bert said that he told his father at the time: "You need to see how people respond to him. When our Den starts to speak at a meeting, you can hear a pin drop. He speaks their language, and they can tell it's coming from the heart. He sets out what we should be doing and why we need to do it."[10]

## Molly's death

In fact, Dennis ended up contesting the Halesowen and Stourbridge parliamentary seat twice in 1974, at the time when Molly, his mother, died in the interval between the February and October general elections. He wanted to stand down but was persuaded to continue out of a sense of duty to Labour and a fear of letting down his team of loyal supporters.

After Dennis's mother passed away, his father and Auntie Kate went on living at Powell Place until his dear aunt eventually died in 1978. In his later years, Bert Senior, now on his own, was taken out every night to Bradley Ex-Servicemen's Club, Bert Junior escorting him there, and Dennis taking him back. Old Bert Senior is still remembered with affection by the Turner and Nash families as a man who was never seen at home, or in public, without boots on his feet, or a cap on his head.

## Love, marriage and family

Dennis met Patricia, his future wife, in the early 1970s. On their first date, he turned up in his battered old Humber Super-Snipe car to take her out to the theatre. She dressed for the occasion in a smart long black and white skirt, but they had not gone very far when the car ran out of petrol. By the time Dennis returned with a can, they had missed their show. Dennis suggested that, as an alternative, they go to the Willenhall Grey Hound Stadium. Pat thoroughly enjoyed the evening, but felt a little overdressed for the dogs.[11]

Since 1967, Pat had been working as a domestic nanny on Long Island in the USA and had only come back home to Wolverhampton for a holiday. Born in 1945 in Millfields Bilston, she had grown up in a pre-fab in Moxley and attended Loxdale Infant and Junior Secondary School in Bilston.[12]

Pat suspected that Dennis had obtained her contact details by way of her father, Joseph Narroway, who worked with Bert Turner Senior, Dennis's father, at the Bilston Steel Works.[13]

Thereafter, Dennis and Pat met on every occasion when she came back from America, but Dennis was insistent that she stay permanently. After nine years abroad, she did indeed return and they were married on 19 June 1976, spending their honeymoon touring the New Forest, Weymouth, Bath and the Isle of Wight.[14]

When they got back, they went to live at 'Ambleside' in King Street, Bradley, close to Dennis's birthplace in Lord Street and his father's home at 6 Powell Place.[15]

### Freddie-dog, the pedigree Labrador

Ken Purchase recounts how on one of his many visits to the Turners' home, Ambleside, in Bradley, he noticed that Dennis and Pat had acquired a new puppy called 'Freddie-dog'. When Ken asked the dog's breed, Dennis told him that Freddie-dog was a pedigree Labrador, a claim that Ken found hard to believe. Remarking that it looked like a mongrel to him, he asked to see its certificate of pedigree, to be told that the paperwork had yet to arrive. When Ken insisted on knowing where the dog had come from, Dennis confided in him that he'd bought it off a gipsy living at a nearby gipsy camp.[16]

When Dennis was asked to confirm this story, he grinned. "I may have told Ken that at the time," he said, "but the dog was a pedigree Labrador and we went to fetch him from a genuine breeder who lived on a farm near Kidderminster", a story his wife, Pat, confirmed independently.[17]

### Favourites

Dennis's favourite meal consisted of lamb chops, Swedes and potatoes, which he always looked forward to eating on his return to Bradley from the culinary desert of London.[18] We might take this opportunity to mention other local delicacies that we have from time to time shared with Dennis, such as faggots and 'pais' at the Springvale club, mini-fish, roe, and chips at Major's in the High Street ('battering the competition since 1976'), and liver and onions with 'a blob and a few' at Jean's Café on the corner of Hargreave Street and the Bilston Road.

In regard to music, Dennis was particularly fond of the human voice and of male voice choirs. He would listen for hours to the singer, Josef Locke, a popular tenor of the 1940s and 50s, remembered mostly for 'Hear my song, Violetta'.[18] His friend, former MP, David Clelland, pointed out that Dennis existed in a kind of musical time warp, and that most of the songs that he liked pre-dated the modern pop era.[19] When on holiday in Benidorm, Dennis would go in search of good vocalists, many of them British, in the night clubs. At home in Wolverhampton, he remained patron of the Orpheus Male Voice Choir until his death.[20] Its president, Liberal Democrat councillor, Malcolm Gwinnett, recalled how Dennis had vigorously supported the choir and frequently joined in the singing from his seat in the audience.[21]

### Brendon and Jenny

Pat and Dennis had two children, Brendon Robert, born on 2nd September 1977, and Jenny Mary, born on 3rd February 1980. Brendon lives next door to his mother in King Street, Bradley, and works as a Personal Fitness Trainer.[22] Jenny has worked as a singer and as a carer in a home. She is married to Mr Steve Mullings, and the couple have a baby daughter called Bella Mary, born in 2011.[23] Dennis was a very proud grandfather and Bella was the apple of his eye.[24]

### Seeing that man

Brendon told us that his father would read 'Monty Monkey' stories to him and his sister, Jen. He recalled that when he was seven years old and about to be sent to bed, his father would put on his jacket and tell him, "I've got to see a man about a dog". Brendon soon came to understand that this meant that his father was going out to work at the Springvale Sports and Social Club. Determined to stay with his father, he would wait for a few minutes after he left, then open the front door and run all the way to the club by himself, a distance of about one mile. When he turned up at the club, his father would grin, telephone his mother, and keep him with him, before taking him home at the end of the evening. Brendon admitted that these occasions became something of a habit, but felt that they illustrated his father's patience, tolerance and affection towards him.[25]

Jenny recalled the impact of the club on family life. Her father would come home late almost every evening.[26] Even on Christmas Day, the club would take precedence and family celebrations would start late.[27] As a young girl, she had believed in Father Christmas, but on being taken to see him, she had become very confused when the man dressed up in the red costume turned out to look very like her father. She had tried to stay awake on Christmas Eve to check out the real Father Christmas, but had fallen asleep before he showed up.[28]

Experience at the club with her father, however, had led to her taking up singing. She attributed her self-assurance when standing and singing in front of an audience to her father's example. He had encouraged her to take the mike at karaoke evenings at the club and other venues, and urged her to cut her own CD.[29]

**Family holidays**

Both Brendon and Jenny were keen to mention how much they had enjoyed their family holidays. Their childhood vacations were usually spent in the United Kingdom, often in Weymouth, or at Aunty Beryl's caravan in Tywyn.[30]

Jenny spoke of the idyllic holidays spent as a little girl in Weymouth, when she and her father would play clock golf and fish for baby crabs on the sea shore. She had become very upset when her dad joked that they should take their bucket-full of crabs home for cooking and eating. She loved animals dearly, and never could understand why he would laugh when she insisted on burying ants that had been trodden on by accident.[31]

Dennis refused to visit Spain under fascist rule and, even after General Franco died in 1975, he was reluctant at first to go there on holiday. Only when the children became teenagers, did the Turners begin to take vacations in Spain like other local families.[32]

Brendon recalled a fortnight spent in Marbella when he and his friend, together with Dennis and Bert, put out from the shore in two pedalos. The sea suddenly became very rough and Brendon's pedalo overturned, forcing him and his companion to abandon the craft and swim ashore. With much emotion, other family members gathered on the beach, screaming for Dennis and Bert to come in immediately, as everyone in the family knew they could not swim. Pedalling slowly and calmly back, the brothers couldn't see what all the fuss was about, a story Brendon tells to illustrate his father and uncle's fearlessness. [33]

In later years, the extended Turner family – Bert and Kath and children, Dennis and Pat and children – would take holidays together in places such as Lanzarote, Majorca, and Tenerife. Dennis was very much a family man.[34]

# Chapter 6

## Saving the steel works

### Joint Union Action Committee

Dennis regards his struggle to prevent the closure of the Bilston steel works as the most momentous event of his life. Lord Beswick, appointed by the Conservatives but kept on by the Labour government, concluded that it was uneconomical to continue making steel by the open-hearth method and opted for a policy of progressively closing furnaces of this kind at steel plants across the country.[1]

The employees at Bilston recognised almost immediately the implications of this decision for the future of their works. In 1973, a meeting was called of all the unions at the plant to launch an active campaign to ensure the plant's survival. An action committee was formed of representatives of the Iron and Steel Trades Confederation (ISTC) to which the vast majority of steel workers including Dennis belonged, the TGWU, the AEUW, the UCATT, the Blastfurnacesmen's Union, and SEMA (managers' union) to save the works and the jobs it provided. Dennis, who was only 31 at the time, was elected chair of this joint union action committee with Reg Turley as vice chair.[2]

In choosing Dennis to front the committee, the shop stewards were already aware of his formidable oratorical skills. He had, after all, been selected to address an ISTC conference, attended by a youthful Prince Charles, which was aimed at introducing the future king to the ways of the trade unions.[3]

The overriding purpose of the committee, reflecting Dennis's socialist principles, was to safeguard jobs, earnings, and the standard of living of the workers, not only for their own sake, but for future generations living in the Black Country. It was decided from the outset that the campaign would be focused on the survival of the plant and its jobs – not on the level of compensation to be won by agreeing to the closure. Dennis insisted on a two-part resolution: to fight to keep open the plant and, only when that was finally lost, to pursue any other material interest, a position maintained unwaveringly for five years of the six-year campaign.[4]

Dennis recognised early on that the fight was not about jobs as such, but about the future economic viability of the Bilston plant. It was indeed profitable, having achieved a £19 million surplus in 1973. Bilston had important technical and economic features that made it different from other plants. It was essential for these to be brought to the fore. For example, the Bilston blast furnace produced 50 per cent of its own electricity.[5]

## Double-end firing

An ingenious blast-furnace engineer – Arthur Latham – had devised a system of double-end firing with blasts of oxygen to achieve significantly higher temperatures in the open-hearth furnaces, enabling them to produce a heat of steel in half the time. Monty Finniston, Chairman of the British Steel Corporation came to Bilston to see the double firing in operation, but the decision had already been taken to commit to a massive national investment in the alternative electric arc technology used for secondary steel making. Double-end firing was abandoned.[6]

## Feasibility study

To press home the economic case for keeping the steel works open, the joint union action committee persuaded four local institutions: the West Midlands County Council, Wolverhampton Borough Council, Wolverhampton Polytechnic, and Bilston College of Further Education, to come together to commission the University of Aston to mount a feasibility study of the economic viability of the Bilston steel works. Undoubtedly facilitated by Dennis's elected positions, the two councils voted £12,500 each to support the study, which showed indeed that the plant was viable and that the greater economy of the Black Country depended on it remaining open, a prediction that turned out to be true, as unemployment rose to 25 per cent of the adult population with the factory closures of the 1980s.[7]

## Worker take-over

During the course of the struggle, the management of British Steel sought to reduce the number of furnaces in operation at Bilston from four to three, which certainly would have destroyed the economic viability of a demonstrably profitable enterprise. At this stage, the workers decided to intervene en masse to keep the furnaces functioning, taking over the management of the site in the process.

Dennis marched with 500 steel workers through A Gate and along A Road to the furnaces, where they proceeded to re-brick the G furnace that was under threat, and fired it up, bringing it back fully into service for a further eighteen months.[8] Dennis recounts how he was about to be stopped by white-collar health and safety officials on the grounds that the workforce was not insured. But, on the previous day, he had taken out an insurance policy at the Co-op for 50 workers and, much to management annoyance, was able to produce the certificate to prove it.[9]

## National campaign

Dennis saw the need to make the fight for the Bilston steel works into a national campaign, with Bilston becoming a symbol of the struggle for the steel industry as a whole. The action committee put on coaches to take the Bilston workers down to London, where they held a mass lobby of parliament, and then proceeded to the headquarters of the British Steel Corporation in Grosvenor Place next to Buckingham Palace. At 250-strong crowd of steel workers visited the Fleet Street offices of the major national newspapers, overwhelming their reception areas and demanding to see industrial correspondents to make their case.[10]

At parliament, the Bilston steel workers met with Gerald Kaufman, the minister with the steel brief in the Department of Industry, from 1975 to 1979. Along with other MPs, Kaufman listened to their case sympathetically and promised to help but, on a later occasion, admitted that his hands were tied. All West Midlands Labour MPs were alerted to the cause. At the newspaper offices, Dennis managed to speak with Paul Routledge, known for his left-wing stance. Paul went on to write in support of the Bilston workers' case.[11]

In Wolverhampton, the trades council threw its weight behind the steel workers' struggle and, when the steel workers went on strike, workers at other local factories, such as GKN Sankey, withdrew their labour in sympathy.[12]

## Redundancy

At headquarters, senior ISTC officials, under the leadership of Bill Sirs, their general secretary, became increasingly concerned that the campaign to save the industry had become almost totally focussed on Bilston. They instructed the joint union action committee to turn its attention to winning compensation for those about to lose their jobs. Management's first offer was for 20 weeks' redundancy money, but the committee succeeded in negotiating a total of 48 weeks pay, small compensation, as they saw it, for the loss of so many people's livelihoods.[13]

The settlement included a generous education and training package for redundant workers who wished to avail themselves of university or college courses in pursuit of a new career.[14]

Dennis's part in the struggle to save the Bilston steel works is commemorated in the third panel on the left-hand side of a frieze, sponsored by the Black Country Development Corporation, and displayed on the old footbridge at Wolverhampton railway station. It pictures a grey-haired Dennis in a red tie, standing near to the image of a steel plant and reading a newspaper with the headline, 'Fairwell Elisabeth'. In the authors' opinion, the artist hasn't achieved an instantly-recognisable likeness.

## The National Steel Strike 2 January-3 April 1980

The last steel billet was cast at Bilston on 12 April 1979, and 'Big Lizzy', the blast furnace, was demolished on 5 October 1980. This was not quite the end of the road, as around 600 workers were kept on at the rolling mills for a further three years. When the Conservative government of Mrs Thatcher came to power in 1979, the Iron and Steel Trades Confederation, together with the National Union of Blastfurnacemen, realised that they had an even greater fight on their hands to safeguard their industry and their members' jobs.

At the tail end of 1979, the British Steel Corporation reported half-year losses of £146m, the Bilston plant had already closed, and Consett in County Durham was also under threat. The Conservative government was promising to privatise the industry which had been nationalised only twelve years previously. In addition, British Steel was only prepared to offer steel workers a pay rise of 2 per cent, when the rate of inflation was running at 17 per cent. In this adverse political climate, Bill Sirs, general secretary of the ISTC, reluctantly called a strike for the 2nd of January 1980, giving the bosses a month to stock up, an opportunity they took advantage of.

## Strike Co-ordination Committee

Dennis was made chair of the ISTC West Midlands Strike Co-ordination Committee, which had the objective of making sure that the strike remained solid, pickets were in place, and no steel got moved or supplied.[15] At one stage, steel workers, ten per cent of them female, were sent down from the North East to help with the picketing. The ISTC brought out its 90,000 workers and the National Union of Blastfurnacemen a further 13,000, of the 150,000 staff employed by British Steel. The stoppage also affected the 35 private steel companies. To stop the supply of steel, companies receiving supplies from stockholders and importers were heavily picketed around the clock. Dennis tells how, on one occasion, he stood on the picket line with Brendon, his four-year old son, strapped in his push chair.[16]

## Confrontation with Sir Keith Joseph

In the middle of the strike, on the 22nd February 1980, when Dennis learned that Sir Keith Joseph, the Conservative Secretary of State for Industry, was visiting Birmingham, he took a delegation to the Edgbaston Conservative Rooms to lobby him, with little success, although a splendid photograph was taken of the event.[17] Joseph was already softening up the nationalised industries for privatisation by bringing in managers from the private sector.

## Dealing with the strike breakers

The strike committee developed new tactics to deal with strike-breaking lorry drivers, who ran into, and through the picket lines in order to load and unload. One technique was to pile workers onto the weighbridges when the lorry drivers tried to weigh out.[18] In one picket-line altercation, Dennis's brother, Bert, was arrested and kept in a cell overnight, to be let out the following morning.[19]

## Pay rise

The strike was called off when the workers were offered a 16-per-cent pay rise in exchange for agreeing to a change in working practices for greater productivity. It had lasted thirteen weeks. Incensed by the attempts to break the strike, the strike co-ordinating committee was not prepared to let the matter rest there. An inter-union meeting of all shop stewards was called to establish a committee of investigation into those transport companies which had instructed their drivers to cross the picket lines. Lorry drivers were blacklisted, with union members refusing to load or unload their vehicles. The thirteen or so companies implicated were invited to send representatives to the committee to explain and apologise for their behaviour. Those who refused to comply found it difficult to operate and contracts were not renewed, with one or two hauliers forced out of business altogether.[20]

The steel strike of 1980 has been variously judged. The outcome maintained wage levels at just about the same rate as inflation, but British steel making went into terminal decline. Later, in the summer of 1980, the Consett Steel Works in County Durham closed and the South Wales steel workers went on to short time. The strike is believed to have delayed the Conservative government's attack on jobs and living standards until its second term in 1983, and its privatisation of the steel industry, in the name of 'market-place discipline', until 1988.

## The effects on the community of unemployment

Dennis's experience of the closure of the steel works and his subsequent redundancy became indelibly etched into his consciousness, to emerge in the context of a notable speech on poverty he made in the House of Lords on the 8th of May 2008:

Drawing attention to the importance of full employment for tackling poverty and improving life chances, he described how the mass unemployment of the 1980s had affected him and his local community:

"I was one of the three million unemployed at the time. Our Bilston steel works was closed with the loss of 2,300 jobs. Factory after factory went out of existence, and 40 per cent of the Black Country's manufacturing base was wiped away. Levels of unemployment ran at 30 per cent, and in some streets it was as high as 50 per cent. Some 35 per cent of our young people were denied their first opportunity of employment since leaving school. Training places were almost non-existent and the careers service was moribund. A depressing sense of hopelessness and despair pervaded our whole community. Soon poverty made its degrading presence felt, and for many human beings, life chances were abruptly truncated at a crucial stage in their lives. Sadly for others, their life chances ebbed away at the moment of their worklessness, never again to return."[21]

Seldom was heard in the Lords a more authentic voice of a man who had witnessed first hand the deleterious effects on his home town of unemployment. Later, an obituary for Dennis in The Times was to describe

63

him as 'one of a dying breed' of parliamentarians who, rather than attempt to hide his background as a former steel worker, simply 'gloried in it'[22]. His profound empathy for working people, with whom he still identified, made it far more than this.

# Chapter 7

## Dove on a dustcart

### Springvale Co-operative Sports and Social Club

When the Bilston steel works finally closed in 1980, it left a huge geographical and social void in the Bilston community – a derelict site of 250 acres, and a large number of redundant workers, many too old to entertain any prospect of further employment. Among the works' assets was a sports and social club, built in 1942, at the height of the second world war, to assist the steel works' 24-hour production by maintaining the workers' morale with a continuous flow of draught beer. The club was situated on four acres of land, with football pitches, tennis courts, a bowling green, and a rifle range.

Dennis, along with other redundant steel workers, came up with the idea of retaining the site on behalf of the Bilston community.[1] Spacious and well-appointed, the building had a ball room with a capacity to hold 250 people, a stage and balcony, and a couple of bars. Other rooms included a concert room, a lounge, a snooker room with four tables, a library (which could be used as a quiet area, and where chess was played), and a kitchen.

A group of ten people, all previously active in the trade unions' campaign to keep open the works, resolved to form a co-operative to take over the facility which, even as the plant closed, was still being used by the workers and their families. The British Steel Corporation was prepared to let the property to the newly-formed group, and each of its members agreed to invest £2,500 of his redundancy money in the venture.[2]

Bert Turner was able to produce the minutes of the Works Welfare Council Meeting held on the 8th January 1981 at the Social Centre. They mentioned the intention of a consortium set up 'to run the social centre as a co-operative. The building and facilities would be held on lease from the BSC. It was suggested that 31st March 1981 was a convenient date for the transfer. The solicitors for the Consortium and the British Steel Corporation had already met and were keeping constantly in touch with each other with regards to developments in the future'.[3]

## The co-operators

Springvale's ten co-operators were:

John Booth (TGWU)
George Burgess (ISTC)
Graham Fazey (ISTC)
Bob Higgins (ISTC)
Graham Howe (TGWU)
Ian McCulloch (ISTC)
Frank Robinson (UCATT)
Bert Turner (ISTC)
Dennis Turner (ISTC)
Ted Wall (ISTC)

All were prepared to back the scheme with £2,500 of their own money (which for a redundant worker in 1981 would have been considered a very large sum, indeed).[4] Largely self-selected by their six-year campaign against the closure of the steel works, they not only invested their redundancy pay, but gave their energy and enthusiasm unstintingly to the project.[5]

The group approached Mervyn Williams, a solicitor and former town clerk of Bilston Borough Council, to draw up an agreement and constitution of co-operation. These were duly completed and signed in the financial year 1981-82.[6] The co-operators all shared the same philanthropic attitude to co-operation, seeing it more as a contribution to their comrades and the community than as a business venture from which they might profit.[7]

Dennis was selected as chair, a position he retained for 27 years until 2008, when the six original surviving co-operators handed over the Springvale Sports and Social Club to the long-established much larger Mid-Counties Cooperative Society.[8]

The Springvale Co-operative could never afford to retain many full-time paid staff, and most tasks were performed on a voluntary basis by the co-operators. Ted Wall, who was 63, and near to retirement age, was made the club manager. Dennis provided overall strategic direction and drive. Each co-operator took a lead on a different aspect of the club's activities: for example, John Booth looked after the tote, George Burgess took on security, Bob Higgins was bar manager, Graham Howe, entertainments manager, and Ian McCulloch organised the indoor sports (snooker, darts, dominoes, crib, etc.). Dennis's brother, Bert, served as the catering manager, his wife, Kath, taking on the role of cook, or chef. Dave Anderson, who had been finance manager at Bilston steel works, but was not one of the ten collaborators, looked after the accounts.[9]

**At the heart of the community**

The vital first task of the new Springvale Co-operative was to make sure that the people and civic societies of Bilston were made aware of the social facilities and the readiness with which they might be accessed by all, in contrast to some of the existing clubs in the town, which still restricted membership on grounds of race, gender and age. From the start, Springvale was made open to all, with pensioners, sporting organisations, choirs, discussion circles, trade unions, Scouts, Boys' Brigade, and other interest groups, encouraged to join en masse, a marketing campaign that met with remarkable success.

The club very soon became the social and political hub for the whole of Bilston and south-east Wolverhampton. On Friday night, members of the South-East Constituency Labour Party, councillors and hangers-on would meet over a pint, engage in congenial conversation, and let their hair down.

The traditional Black Country fare served in the club often provided the backdrop to Black Country tall stories and humour. On the rare occasions Dennis told us a joke, we recall him recounting to us the story of the three Bilston bears: father, mother and 'babby' bear, with 'faggots and pais' substituted for the customary porridge, and a cat burglar for poor little Goldilocks, who was credited with stealing the bear family's TV.

One joke that resonated particularly well with the Friday-night circle went as follows. Feeling hungry after an evening of energetic canvassing in Hartlepool, Peter Mandelson and Tony Blair visit the local chippy to buy fish and chips. Peter Mandelson notices a steel pan of mushy peas, and points to it, declaring in a plummy voice: "I'll take a portion of your guacamole, too". Those club-goers, who understood what 'guacamole' was, found this apocryphal story irresistible and repeated it to their friends.

Other memorable entertainment included the 'Springvale Follies', and its off-shoot, 'the War Babes', who sang nostalgic jazzy second-world-war numbers.[10]  Maureen Harris and Patty Howe may still be going strong. Most senior citizens in Bilston will recall the popular tea dances, held in the afternoon in the ball room. At Christmas, the kitchen used to cater for 1,000 old-age pensioners, serving a four-course lunch for 200, five days in a row.

Dennis believed that, following the closure of the steel works, the Springvale club had made an immense contribution to the sense of local community, to the maintenance of social cohesion in the area, and to tackling the challenges still faced by the neighbourhood.[11]

**People's March for Jobs**

On the evening of the 14th May 1981, after a rally in St Peter's Square, in the centre of Wolverhampton, Springvale played host to participants in the People's March for Jobs, held to highlight the rising unemployment rates, and intended to evoke the jobless marches of the 1930s. About 280 marchers started out from Liverpool. They ended up a month later at a rally, 150,000 strong, in Hyde Park. The march was headed by a disabled person in a wheelchair pushed by colleagues. When the marchers arrived in Wolverhampton, they were addressed by Tony Benn and entertained by the Spinners, the Liverpool folk group. Afterwards, they were accommodated overnight in the Springvale Club.[12]

Dennis, hoping to contribute to the spirit of the occasion, bought a white dove from a local pet shop and, to great applause, release the bird into the sky as the march was about to move off in the direction of Walsall, on the next leg of the journey. After rising a yard or so into the air, the dove promptly landed on a municipal dustcart passing by on the road, and was carried out of sight amid much ribald laughter.[13]

In parliament, Labour MP David Winnick pointed out that 6,000 people were joining the dole queues everyday, while 400,000 had been out of work for more than twelve months. When Mrs Thatcher, the Prime Minister, asked whether she would receive the organisers of the march when they arrived in London, she gave a one-word answer: "no".

**Youth Training Scheme**

As youth unemployment rose to ever greater heights, the Co-operators decided to extend Springvale's activities to include a Youth Training Scheme, run from the buildings of the former Bilston Steel Corporation's training centre, situated at the rear of the club.[14] Supported by the Manpower Service Commission (MSC), this arrangement lasted for five or six years, and was managed by Dave Anderson, ably assisted by a team of trainers, including the very able Sue Kunynec.

**Race horses**

The club catered for a range of Black Country social, cultural and sporting activity. A consortium of members and friends bought a race horse, Springvale Bid, but it fell at Worcester and had to be destroyed.[15] Jenny, Dennis's daughter, a young girl at the time, described how she wept uncontrollably as the screen was put round the beast.[16]

A second horse, Springvale Crusader, raced in the Midlands and the North, with notable wins at Perth and Ayr. Central television made a film of Springvale supporters taking a coach to Uttoxeter, to watch their horse run. Crusader came in third, amid much jubilation. The race horse became a great favourite of the racing fraternity.[17]

## The Parliamentary Co-operative Group

Dennis never waned in his promotion of the values of co-operatives as a superior form of social organisation. Between 1992 and 1994, he chaired the Parliamentary Co-operative Group, consisting of Co-operative MPs, and played an active part in the Co-operative Party's annual national conferences.

Dennis continued to believe that co-ops had an important role to play in the development of the economy, but felt that the very success of local government in providing housing, schools, community and leisure centres, sporting facilities and allotments, etc., undermined the case for a co-operative delivery of social services. He was fearful that co-operatives might be encouraged by local authorities to take on the provision of services as a convenient cost-cutting exercise, thus doubly disadvantaging the poorest communities.[18]

As a sports and social club, the Springvale Co-op triggered another of Dennis's lasting interests. He became secretary and a firm supporter of the All-Party Parliamentary Group for Non-Profit-Making Members' Clubs, which had the objective of supporting non-profit-making members' clubs around the country.[19]

The Co-operative Party, the Springvale Co-op, and the Co-operative movement as a whole, formed an essential element of Dennis's life and philosophy. However inadvertently it came to pass, The Times obituary for Lord Bilston misrepresented the character and motivation of the man entirely when it claimed that 'out of the closure' of the steel works, 'a group of workers invested their redundancy payments to set up a successful sports and leisure company, of which Turner was chairman'.[20] This statement carries the unfortunate implication that Dennis was acting merely as a businessman with an eye to profiting from the assets of a privatised industry - a British equivalent of a Russian oligarch!

# Chapter 8

## An extraordinary educational experiment

Of all Dennis's considerable achievements, one in particular –the creation of Bilston Community College - illustrates the originality of his thinking on social policy, his skill in convincing others of the value of what he had in mind, his ability to assemble a team with the resources to deliver it, and his success in creating a new radical institution and practice on the ground. Paradoxically, the college's subsequent liberation from local authority control, runaway expansion, catastrophic financial crisis, and closure as a 'failing institution' constituted the low point of his political life. Expressed metaphorically, Dennis viewed Bilston Community College as his baby daughter. He was as proud as punch when she came of age and utterly devastated when she died on him. Dennis's political stature and tenacity, however, is demonstrated by his continued commitment to, and efforts on behalf of the broader national movement for adult, community, and further education.

### Youth unemployment

The downturn in the economy of the 1980s and the rising in unemployment, especially among young people, led Dennis to assemble a partnership of all the bodies which might contribute to the solution. This went well beyond the confines of the local council's various departments, to include the Wolverhampton Polytechnic, the further education colleges, and government departments, such as the Department of Employment (D of E), the Manpower Services Commission (MSC), and the Department of Health and Social Security (DHSS). In many ways, the emergent Youth Unemployment Action Group might be seen as a precursor of the Local Strategic Partnership.

With the heavy engineering industries of the Black Country in the doldrums, young people not only found themselves out of a job, but unable to make use of the apprenticeships and other established ways of acquiring technical skills for their self-advancement. Further education colleges were forced to close

73

City and Guild and ONC courses, as the number of day-release students fell. Simultaneously, the young unemployed multiplied inexorably. Meanwhile, more young people chose to stay on at school beyond the statutory school leaving age, often following sixth-form studies unsuited to their needs.

## Duplication of sixth-form provision

In Bilston, the situation had been complicated by an earlier comprehensivisation of secondary schools, involving the closure of the selective boys' and girls' grammar schools, and the creation of an open-access sixth-form centre on the doorstep of the further education college, resulting in an unnecessary and wasteful duplication of sixth-form provision. Established with the primary purpose of doing away with selection at the age of 11 and the tripartite system, the Bilston Sixth-Form Centre could only ever offer provision for a limited section of 16-to-19 year olds and, indeed, highlighted still further the divisions at sixteen between academic, technical, craft, and operative routes into employment.[1]

## Tertiary proposals

With increasing numbers of sixteen-year-olds unable to find a job, or find their way into education or training, Dennis, as chair of Wolverhampton Council's Further Education Committee, came up with a new concept and plan - initially intended only to apply to the Bilston area. It was to amalgamate the sixth-form centre, the further education college, and any other related or free-standing educational, training and leisure facilities for young people, into a 'tertiary' or 'community' college.[2] Tertiary (or third stage) education meant providing a full range of academic and vocational courses, offered on a full, part-time, or evening basis, after the school leaving age at 16. Dennis had a personal interest in Bilston's educational arrangements, having experienced at first hand its strengths and weaknesses. His entire formal education had taken place at Stonefield Secondary Modern School and Bilston College of Further Education, where he had followed a course in office accounts.

The new Bilston Community College was seen as the means of improving staying-on rates, of raising educational standards for the 16-to-19 age group as a whole, and of increasing the numbers progressing to higher education – which for the Bilston area were disproportionately low. The college offered an alternative to a wasteful 'tripartite' system of 16-to-19 education, provided separately in 11-to-18 school sixth forms, 16-to-19 sixth-form colleges, and colleges of further education.

## Open access

True to Dennis's socialist principles and experience of failing the eleven plus, the new college had to be 'open access', in the sense that it would make provision for anyone of any age or social-class background who could benefit from its education programmes and facilities. The aim was to gear courses to individual need, rather then to exclude students who had so far failed to make the grade at secondary school. Traditional education had been selective and elitist, not only erecting barriers to study, but inculcating the belief among large sections of the population that they were not sufficiently worthy or capable of study.[3]

Open-access education also implied the redistribution of resources in favour of those who had gained least from education in the past.

## Equal opportunity

The new college was to lay great emphasis on equal opportunity. Dennis was insistent that it operated on the principle that all human beings had an inherent worth and were educable, irrespective of differences of social class, gender, disability, age and race. In 1989, the widespread disadvantage and discrimination in the education system as a whole, as well as in the wider society, presented a major challenge of converting a principle such as this into a routine college practice.[4]

In response, Bilston Community College began to develop a range of so-called 'access courses', to help students enter higher education, specialist occupational areas, or jobs traditionally dominated by men or women, such as construction or nursery nursing. And it massively expanded courses for young people with special needs. Dennis, as chair of the council's special education committee, took a particular interest in this facility.

In regard to equality of opportunity, the college strove to expand student numbers and to ensure unemployed people, people from working-class backgrounds, women, ethnic minorities, and those with disabilities, were made welcome, offered suitable courses, and obtained their fair share of the facilities on offer.

## Dennis's support for further education

As the long-standing chair of Wolverhampton Council's Further Education Committee in the 1970s and early 80s, Dennis not only took the far-reaching Bilston tertiary education plan to committee and full council for approval, but drove it through, despite attempts to oppose, or water down, the proposals from unenthusiastic officers and councillors, still wedded to the traditional selective and elitist ideas of the past.[5]

As the college's founding father and its steadfast political patron, Dennis was persuaded to join the board of Bilston Community College when, in 1992, following the Further and Higher Education Act, it became an independent corporation, no longer attached to or funded by the local authority. He served on the board, as vice-chair, until 1999, when it became part of the borough-wide Wolverhampton College.

## Ten successful years

For the first ten years of its existence, Bilston Community College more than fulfilled Dennis's expectations. The college expanded student numbers and increased local community participation in educational initiatives on a grand scale, taking full advantage of the independence from local authority control granted to it by the Education Reform Act 1988 and the 'formula funding' introduced by the Further Education Funding Council after 1992.

While under local authority control, the college had only been able to grow in size within the Wolverhampton area, and in accordance with the budget it was allocated by the council, thus encouraging it to focus its attention on local people previously uninvolved in education and training. With formula funding, however, the college received money for every new enrolment and was able to recruit students from outside of the borough.

### From ethics to finance

Imperceptibly, the college switched from being ethically driven by its equal opportunity and open access policies to being financially driven, for ever maintaining and increasing its income by enrolling larger and larger numbers of students, whatever they chose to study, and wherever they lived.

The rapidly-expanding enrolments fooled most spectators, including Dennis and the college governors, into believing that the college was fulfilling its aim of extending educational opportunity, whereas, in many cases, it was merely subsidising activities that would have taken place anyway, without the college's intervention.

### Franchising

The college relied increasingly on reaching its ambitious enrolment targets by entering into partnerships with other providers through a system of 'franchising'. In essence, this meant enrolling members or clients of other organisations and paying in return those agencies an element of the money received by the college from the Further Education Funding Council.

In this way, between 1994 and 1997, the college expanded from 11,000 to 55,000 enrolments. In common with other governors, Dennis welcomed the dramatic expansion in enrolments as a demonstration of the effectiveness of the Bilston approach to adult and community education.

The Further Education Funding Council encouraged franchising at this time as the principal means of achieving the ambitious targets it had agreed with the Conservative government, which gained kudos from the apparent exponential growth of education and training opportunities.

Under the label of education and training, people participating in all kinds of activity, such as bible reading, horse riding, judo, and marching bands, were enrolled as college students. Participants in these activities were signed up en masse, with each enrolment counting as a quantum of funding. The college then made efforts to put in place formal syllabuses and qualifications to give the process a greater semblance of legitimacy.

## International ambitions

Believing that the college expansion represented a form of economic development and regeneration, the principal sought to spread the message of the college's success, not just in the United Kingdom, but abroad in Eastern Europe and various other countries in the Caribbean, Africa and India. The college's international agenda resonated naturally with Dennis's own beliefs in international solidarity and overseas development. He saw the overseas projects as a means of educating Bilston students about other racial and ethnic groups and nationalities, and of helping to eliminate the vestiges of pernicious racism which had endured in Wolverhampton since the days of Enoch Powell.

Some of the early international projects were very successful, particularly one in the Caribbean to build hurricane-proof schools, which was run in conjunction with the Monserrat Department of Education. Without a constant stream of international developmental funding, however, it was difficult to see how activities of this kind could be sustained. It was apparent that the college would not be able to recover the full cost of these ventures from the countries most in need of education and development, as they were not in a position to pay.

## Bilston: the hole in the doughnut

The pursuit of franchising contracts in other parts of the country and the focus on international educational projects, such as the Moscow Business College, resulted inevitably in the college experiencing what might at best be referred to as 'mission drift'. The extent of the country-wide franchising soon led to the neglect and under-funding of the college's traditional courses and of its outreach work in the local Bilston community, creating a kind of educational 'doughnut', with a dearth or 'hole' in provision occurring at the centre, in the neighbourhood of Bilston itself.

The increased student numbers, presented as evidence of success, did not necessarily imply greater opportunities for the disadvantaged groups the college claimed to be serving. Young people in urban Bilston were not benefiting in any way from the franchised horse-riding courses being run in the rural south-west. Few people recognised the doughnut effect before 1996. College vice principal, Frank Reeves, eventually felt obliged to confide in Dennis his fear that large-scale franchising was impacting adversely on community education in the heartland of Bilston. Dennis accepted immediately the truth of this analysis, and expressed his surprise and regret. But it was only after the college's finance director, Paul Goddard-Patel, revealed the perilous state of the college's finances that the governors woke up to the unfolding tragedy. Dennis was utterly dismayed that the college he had created had ended up failing the people of Bilston.

## Nemesis under Labour

The road which the college principal had chosen to follow led inevitably through a forest of self-deception towards a financial precipice. Until as late as 1997, officials at the Further Education Funding Council, the college principal, and most of the college's senior staff believed firmly in franchising as an effective means of delivering further education and occupational training to large numbers of people. Junior staff who challenged the orthodoxy were regarded as disloyal and subversive.

Realising eventually that the much-heralded expansion in further education provision under the Conservative ministry was little more than an illusion, the Further Education Funding Council itself attempted to rein in the major franchising institutions and put its house into order for the incoming Labour administration. It tightened the rules relating to franchising, launched a series of audits and inspections, and terminated the so-called 'demand-led' element, paid as an incentive to colleges to expand their provision. In 1997, Bilston found its unit allocation cut by almost one fifth. The Funding Council began to show intense interest in the college's finances, conducting a detailed audit of its franchising arrangements and financial forecasts.

At this point, the principal, to the surprise and disappointment of many, announced that he was standing down as college chief executive, and taking a back seat until his retirement at the end of 1998. Dennis saw the principal's action as a betrayal of the trust he had placed in him, comparing it later to a captain abandoning his crew and ship as soon as he sailed into stormy water.[6]

Estimates of the amount of money the college owed rose recurrently from three, to five, to nine, and finally, to eleven million pounds, as the Funding Council disallowed and reclaimed funding it had given to run franchised courses, year upon year, back into the distant past, despite the fact that annual accounts had been signed off regularly by Deloitte Touche, the college's external auditors.

George Mudie, the Under-Secretary for the Department for Education and Employment from 1998 to 1999, announced that the Labour government would see to it that failing colleges were closed and their governors sacked. Later in 1999, parliament gave the Funding Council powers to wind up Bilston Community College and hand over its assets to the neighbouring Wulfrun College, from which was created the current Wolverhampton College.

## Undiminished support for further education

Dennis was heartbroken, but the sinking of his flag-ship community college did not dim his passionate interest in community and further education. Undeterred, he went on chairing the All-Party Parliamentary Group for Further Education which he had set up when he had first entered parliament, and lobbied ministers ceaselessly on behalf of the colleges[7] (see also Chapter 10).

In his speech to the Lords on the 28th June 2007, Dennis welcomed the government's commitment to further education, signalled by increases it had made to funding, and he praised Prime Minister Gordon Brown's proposals that businesses, universities, colleges and the voluntary sector should be brought together and that every school should be formally linked to a college or university, as part of the agenda for all 14-to-19 year olds.[8] Dennis saw further education as being crucial to the success of the prime minister's ambition to ensure that all young people stayed in education and training until they were eighteen, and that they were all given access to personal learning relevant to their needs, and an offer of an apprenticeship or place in a college or university.[9]

Dennis went on to describe how further education colleges were succeeding, not only in helping the country to meet its global economic challenges by improving skills, but in transforming the lives of individuals by giving them the self-assurance and motivation to make a contribution to their own communities. He asked the House "to remember that 'skills' is not just an amorphous name given to the need to address the global economic challenge. It is also about individuals' personal ambitions and achievements".[10]

## Education as an answer to poverty

In a memorable speech on poverty in 2008, Dennis expressed, even more forcibly, his belief in the power of education to reduce unemployment and poverty, and to transform local communities:

"Education, at every stage of development, imbues empowerment in the individual, the family and the community, transforming lives with knowledge, and opening up opportunities for economic and social advancement. Therein rests the real challenge of combating poverty through improving life chances." [11]

# Chapter 9

## Soft-shoe shuffle into parliament

### Bob Edwards, MP

Bob Edwards was elected as a Labour Co-op MP for the Bilston constituency in the 1955 general election, succeeding Will Nally. The constituency was abolished in 1974, but Bob was subsequently selected as the Labour candidate for the new Wolverhampton South East constituency, which covered much of the same area. In 1983, at the age of 78, he became the oldest MP in the House, a status he retained until he stood down at the election of 1987, to be replaced by Dennis, his close friend, confidant, and favoured successor.

As a leading member of the Labour Party in Bilston and Wolverhampton, Dennis worked closely with Bob, the constituency MP, and Councillor Mary Pointon, Bob's election agent, becoming what might best be described as Bob's 'aide de camp', especially at election time.[1]

Bob and Dennis became close friends. Bob stayed with Dennis and made 'Ambleside', in Bradley, his home in the constituency. 'Ambleside' became his permanent address when his wife, May, died in 1970.[2]

As a former member of the Independent Labour Party, Bob was a revered elder statesman of the left. Bob became Dennis's political mentor and guide, while Dennis was treated by Bob as a surrogate son.[3] Bob and Dennis shared much in common. Bob was the son of a Liverpool docker, Dennis of a steel worker. At 22, Bob was the youngest candidate to stand for Liverpool City Council, to which he was elected in 1932. Dennis was 23 when he became the youngest-ever councillor on the Wolverhampton Borough Council in 1966. More fundamentally, they both shared a visceral urge to improve the lot of the working-class masses from whom they were sprung.[4]

Bob had a formidable socialist track record. As a young man, he had led an Independent Labour Party youth delegation to the Soviet Union, where he met Joseph Stalin, Vyacheslav Molotov, and León Trotsky. During the General Strike, he had carried messages between the unions and the TUC. In the 1930s, he went to Spain to fight fascism, serving as captain in the ILP contingent of the POUM on the Aragon Front, along with George Orwell and Bob Smillie. As a member of the Independent Labour Party before the second world war, he had contested three parliamentary seats, all unsuccessfully, and he had chaired the ILP from 1943 to 1948. Bob was a passionate internationalist, believing fervently that the workers of the world should unite, a well-worn maxim which, nevertheless, helped to fashion Dennis's attitudes to Britain's overseas aid programme, the Empire and Commonwealth, relations with Europe, New Commonwealth immigration, Enoch Powell's 'river of blood' rhetoric, racial discrimination, and racism.[5]

**Bob Edwards' views on Europe**

Bob's experiences of Spain, and the consequence of Franco, Mussolini and Hitler's rise to power, made him determined to ensure fascism would never again be allowed to pass, and to take any step necessary to secure a permanent peace in Europe. For Bob, this meant support for the 1957 Treaty of Rome and the European Economic Community, or Common Market (which was renamed the European Community after the Maastricht Treaty of 1993). As a result of Bob's influence, Dennis was always a committed European, campaigning in favour of continued membership when Harold Wilson's Labour government held a referendum on the issue in 1975.[6]

Bob died in 1990 aged 85. In 2009, an officially-authorised history of the British security service (MI5) entitled, *The Defence of the Realm*, written by Christopher Andrew, a Cambridge don, was published. It alleged that Bob Edwards had been a long-term KGB agent.[7] All those who knew Bob Edwards, and were familiar with his background as chair of the Trotskyist-inclined ILP, would have found this suggestion risible. Dennis, as his 'aide de camp', was angered at the character assassination of such a fine socialist.

## The February and October 1974 General Elections for the Halesowen & Stourbridge Constituency

In 1974, Dennis won selection as Labour candidate for the new parliamentary constituency of Halesowen and Stourbridge, fighting both the February and October general elections, as Harold Wilson tried to win the Labour Party a workable parliamentary majority. In a three-way contest against the Conservative, John Stokes, and Liberal, L T Eden, in what appeared to be a conservatively-inclined seat, Dennis, with 33.81 per cent of the vote, lost by 4,649 to Stokes in the February election but, by October, had clawed his way up to 37.6 per cent, losing by a mere 850, in what all parties observed was a hotly-fought and extremely well-organised campaign.

In 1976, Dennis sought selection for the Rotherham by-election, but lost the nomination by six votes to Stanley Crowther. In 1979, he tried to secure the Dudley West constituency, but was beaten in the nomination by one vote by M J Hartley-Brewer, who went on to lose the election and the seat by 1,049 votes to the Conservative, John Blackburn. As a former steel worker, Dennis believed he might just have scraped home in a constituency that had recently seen its own steel works closed: the Round Oak at Brierley Hill.[8]

### MP for Wolverhampton South East, 1987

Bob Edwards had stood successfully for the Labour and Co-operative Party in the Wolverhampton South East constituency from the time it was formed in 1974 until 1983, consistently taking around 55 per cent of the vote until 1983, when his share of the vote fell to 44.7 per cent.

As Bob's favoured successor, Dennis was selected to stand for Labour/Co-op in the 1987 general election against a Conservative, John Mellor, and SDP Liberal Alliance, Richard Whitehouse. That year, the Wolverhampton Labour Party's handling of the McCurbin incident, in which a young black man died while being arrested in a local Next shop, disastrously affected its electoral performance. Nevertheless, Dennis still managed to increase the

Labour vote by 2,300 above its 1983 total and to win a 48.9 per cent share of the vote.

## Soft-shoe shuffle

Dennis remembered with affection the help afforded to him in his parliamentary campaign by Neil Kinnock, the Labour Party Leader at the time. Neil and Dennis developed a dance routine which they called their 'soft-shoe shuffle' and performed it together in Lichfield Street, Wolverhampton, outside the Grand Theatre, to laughter and applause. Recalling the incident, over a quarter of a century later, Neil wrote, "Anyone who missed out on Dennis's preference for laughter above just about any other activity would be missing the best bit. We hardly ever see each other without replaying the soft-shoe shuffle that we performed together in Wolverhampton during an election campaign."

"It raised hoots of amusement then, and, in the august corridors of the House of Lords, it can still get a smile from even the sourest noble peer. It's not exactly Fred Astaire and Ginger Rogers, or even Flanagan and Allan, but the sight of two old gents, humming a tune and synchronising a sprightly step, mystifies the dull and gets giggles from the rest. Dennis's consistently dapper appearance, I must say, gives a touch of class to the event."[9]

## 'Kicking' the Tories

Roger Lawrence, candidate in 1987 for the neighbouring constituency of Wolverhampton South West, describes how he and Dennis used to liaise on Labour's general election campaign in the town. One of the highlights was the Red Wedge tour which came to the Civic Hall. "At the end of the show, Wolverhampton's three Labour candidates were called onto the stage in front of an audience who had been attracted by Captain Sensible and Billy Bragg, rather than by us three stooges. We each said a few words", he recalled, "then Dennis ended by declaring, 'we've got to kick out Thatcher and the Tories'. He simultaneously lifted his foot and gave a mighty kick in the air which a

Welsh fly half would have been proud of. I still don't know how he managed to stay upright and not land on his backside on the stage. Dennis won, but Labour did not."[10]

## Dennis's personal vote

As a conscientious county and borough councillor, constant supporter of Bilston peoples' interests and causes, and the man who had fought to keep open the steel works, Dennis earned the love and appreciation of Wolverhampton people.

Anyone who campaigned with Dennis was aware of his unparalleled personal knowledge of the Bilston wards, and of the concerns of constituents, to the extent that it was rumoured that he knew the names not only of individual electors, but of their children - and their dogs. (The full implication of this anecdote was lost on middle-class party workers, unaware of the esteem in which racing dogs, or greyhounds, were held in 'the promised land'.)

Many years later, Pat McFadden, who succeeded Dennis as MP for Wolverhampton South East, recalled his experience of campaigning alongside Dennis on Bilston home territory: "Rarely could a politician have been so familiar with his constituency. His encyclopaedic knowledge came from a lifetime of living there, an uncanny memory for names and faces, his work as a Betterware salesman, his campaign for the steel works, and the long years he had spent as a councillor and MP. A walk down Bilston High Street with Dennis took a long time, as a constant stream of people came up to say hello, tell him their news, and pass the time of day."[11]

Roger Lawrence, Labour leader of the council, made a similar observation: "Walking through Bilston with Dennis was a never-to-be-forgotten experience. He knew everyone and they all knew him. A cheerful word, or more usually several, was shared with each of them, unless Dennis knew of something requiring a more sombre word, and Dennis did 'sombre' at least as well as 'cheery'. His approach to electioneering probably owed more to the nineteenth century than to New Labour and voter i.d. 'Go and knock this street out,' he would command. 'Which numbers?' I would ask. 'Oh, they're all Labour down there,' he would say. Well, they weren't, as I found out. But Dennis had that confidence. He couldn't believe that anyone from his manor could be anything but Labour!"[12]

They may not have been Labour votes, but they may still have been Turner votes for, over many tears of dedicated work for his constituents, Dennis had developed his own personal vote, variously estimated by local psephologists to be around 500 at ward level, and 3,000 in a general election. While canvassing in the wards of Wolverhampton South East, we have on frequent occasions been asked the name of our candidate and been variously told: "I don't usually vote, unless it's for Dennis Turner", or "I'm a Conservative through and through, but if it's Dennis, he's done a lot round here, and I'll be supporting him". We do not know whether voting for an individual across party lines on this scale is a common phenomenon in other constituencies, but we personally have never encountered it on such a scale elsewhere in a lifetime of knocking on doors at election time.

In successive elections in 1992, 1997, and 2001, until he retired in favour of Pat McFadden in 2005, Dennis managed to ramp up the Labour support on each occasion to 56.7 per cent, 63.7, and 67.4 per cent of the vote.

# Chapter 10

## Steel Man grapples with Iron Lady

### Facing Mrs Thatcher

The general election of 11 June 1987 returned 376 Conservative, 229 Labour, and 22 SDP Liberal Alliance MPs to parliament. Despite the fact that the Labour Party under Neil Kinnock increased its share of the vote by 3.2 per cent and the number of its seats by 20, the Conservatives, led by Mrs Thatcher, won their third consecutive election victory. They had campaigned for lower taxes, a strong economy and defence, in a context in which unemployment had fallen below three million, and inflation to 4 per cent, its lowest point for 20 years. The electorate did not seem to have blamed them for the misery inflicted on millions of working people who had lost not only their jobs but their local industrial heritage and infrastructure. Triumphant in Wolverhampton, Dennis entered parliament in the midst of his party's defeat.

Mrs Thatcher was one of the few people who Dennis saw as an utterly implacable enemy of 'his people', and whom he could never forgive for the damage she had done, as leader of the Conservative Party, to all the causes he held dear. He held her political programme responsible for the high unemployment rates, particularly among young people, for the riots of the 80s, for breaking the back of the trade union movement, for the free-market economics and privatisation of the utilities, including gas, water and electricity, for the growth in indirect taxation, for high interest rates, for embracing militarism and the cold-war policies of Ronald Reagan, and for the US's Cruise and Pershing missiles at Greenham Common, and much more besides. It was no wonder that her professed hatred of socialism and uncompromising style of leadership had led to a Soviet journalist dubbing her 'the Iron Lady', a title she seemed to appreciate.

When Dennis died in 2014, Daniel Wainwright, the political editor of the *Express & Star*, described how he had asked Lord Bilston to accompany him to see the biographical film, 'The Iron Lady', directed by Phyllida Lloyd, in which Meryl Streep played the part of Mrs Thatcher. Dennis, he wrote, "was utterly and completely horrified at how he believed her policies affected manufacturing in the Black Country," but that he had remained "respectful of her belief that she was doing the right thing. He just politely disagreed. He was able to see beyond the iconic figure of hatred she was to those who shared his political views, and recall how he had once asked her about people starving, only for the prime minister to remark that he was 'looking rather well on it,'" a reference to his rather more portly appearance at the time.[1]

In truth, Dennis was instinctively able to distinguish between an act of individual personal kindness and a heartless creed or policy, but his respect for Mrs Thatcher, as a fellow human being and sharp-witted MP, could never extend to her politics. He gave her as good as he got. On one occasion, he took a 22-month-old baby requiring heart surgery along to 10 Downing Street, and roared: "A little girl's come over a 100 miles to see you, Mrs Thatcher!"[2]

**So much in common!**

Dennis told the story of how, after his second day at Westminster, he was waiting at the members' entrance for a taxi to Euston, when he heard a posh melodious voice behind him in the queue asking, "Anyone going north?"

When Dennis indicated that he was going in that direction, the person declared, "I'll share the cab with you, my man!"

In the taxi, the man asked him, "Who are you?"

When Dennis explained he was a Black Country MP, the man expressed his delight: "My goodness! I know the area like the back of my hand. I've taken my narrow boat all over the Black Country on the Birmingham Canal Navigation."

Dennis mentioned in conversation how his grandfather, old Ben Peasley, had been a Black Country boatman, who transported foundry sand from quarries near Tettenhall to foundries in Tipton and Coseley.

"Oh my goodness!" said his travelling companion, "We have so much in common. My grandfather was chairman of the Grand Union Canal Company for 50 years."

Thus, Dennis found himself in the company of Colwyn Jestyn John Philipps, the Viscount St Davids, who lived near Regent's Park and kept his two narrow boats moored nearby on the Grand Union Regent's Canal.

While finding this incident wryly amusing, Dennis thought it captured the essence of his induction as an ordinary Black Country working-class MP into the life of Westminster.[3] The ultimate irony was to occur many years later, with the ejection from the Upper House, under the House of Lords Act 1999, of all but 92 of the hereditary peers and their replacement with life peers, whose number Dennis would eventually join.

### Dennis settles in

David Clelland told us how he had entered parliament at the Tyne Bridge by-election of December 1985, about eighteen months before Dennis, but had been staggered by his colleague's astonishing ability, far surpassing his own, to learn the first names of everyone at the Palace of Westminster, not only of the MPs, but of most of the staff and workers. Dennis also took a keen interest in the parliamentary catering service, pointing out and asking for particular morsels at the service counter and commenting on their quality.

On one occasion, he saw 'oxtail soup' on the menu chalked up on the blackboard in the members' dining room, and ordered a bowl of it for his lunch. He confided in David that it tasted good, but that he was sure it wasn't 'oxtail', but 'French onion'. Returning to the counter for a second helping, he told staff that he liked the soup, but it was definitely not 'oxtail'. Soon after, a manager came over to ask him whether he was satisfied with his meal.

"Yes," he said, "but I do know the difference between 'oxtail' and 'French onion'." She reassured him there was only 'oxtail' on the menu. A little while later, the chef tapped him on the shoulder to confirm once more that the soup he had prepared was 'oxtail'.

Dennis told him firmly, "I do know the difference between 'oxtail' and French onion." The chef inquired whether he might sample a spoonful. After tasting a mouthful, the chef grimaced and apologised. "The stupid girl's been giving you the gravy."[4] When Dennis was asked to confirm David's story, he remembered that the chef on duty that day had been 'Stuart', who was still on the catering staff.[5]

The story illustrates Dennis's early attentiveness to the food served to members, and to the staff who prepared it. It also explains why he was eventually selected to head up the Catering Committee.

**Dennis's maiden speech**

Dennis delivered his maiden speech to the Commons at 8.05pm on the 2nd July 1987.[6] Bruce Grocott, a fellow MP and friend, drew attention to what it revealed about Dennis's character, commitment and purpose.[7] It showed that he had entered parliament to press for the interests of his Black Country constituents in the face of a government which did not understand their needs or aspirations. According to Bruce, Dennis's slightly breathless and rasping delivery only helped to underscore his deep and sincere conviction.

Dennis began by thanking the House for the warm welcome and helpful way he had been treated, but then went on to pay tribute to Bob Edwards, whom he regarded as his mentor: "I come to the House following a legend – the legend of Bob Edwards...a fine parliamentarian, who devoted all his life to the interests of the people. If I can serve the people of my constituency one quarter as well as he did, I should be very pleased".[8]

Dennis then turned his attention to the Conservative government. Many of his constituents "would not comprehend what has been said in the speeches over the past few days". Where he came from, unemployment stood at 25 per cent, and 25,000 people in Wolverhampton were out of work and denied the opportunity to contribute to society, or to receive the rewards arising from it.

"When we talk of unemployment, we must take into account the indignity that comes with it. Independence and freedom have been mentioned often in the past few days. The people whom I represent no longer have the freedom and independence given by the wage packet. A wage packet is important to them, and their dignity, standards and independence are based on that. So I must reconcile freedom and independence with the difficulties and impoverishment in which many of our people have been placed by being out of work and finding it difficult to cope in present circumstances."[9]

Dennis's maiden speech drew attention to the people who had to exist on £39.50 a week, the government's failure to invest in council housing, the thousands of senior citizens and disabled people seeking sheltered accommodation or bungalows, the number reliant on housing benefit and unable to buy a roof over their head, the shortage of hospital beds and emergency treatment, and the reduction in capital grants to schools. He suggested that MPs should come together to start building something better, not only for some of the people, but for all of them, for "that would make a tremendous contribution to the people whom I represent".[10]

**On the opposition benches**

Dennis found himself on the opposition benches for ten long years, serving under three successive opposition leaders: Neil Kinnock, John Smith and Tony Blair, and facing two Tory prime ministers: Margaret Thatcher and John Major.

Mrs Thatcher remained prime minister until 28 November 1990, during which time the rate of unemployment continued to fall, new jobs were created in the retail sector, and property prices began to rise. In the West Midlands, for example, the Merry Hill Shopping Centre opened on the site of a former steelworks and provided 6,000 retail jobs by 1989. Soon after the election, however, Mrs Thatcher's popularity began to wane as she pressed ahead with the poll tax (officially known as the 'community charge'). She was replaced as prime minister by the Chancellor, John Major.

Despite a jump in unemployment in 1991, Major proved popular. When he went to the country in April 1992, he managed unexpectedly to win – albeit with a reduced majority of 21. The Labour defeat led to the resignation of Neil Kinnock and his replacement by John Smith.

Although he won the election, John Major was faced with a series of crises which made it increasingly unlikely the Conservatives would remain in power the next time round. The pound sterling had to be taken out of the European exchange rate mechanism, interest rates increased, and the Tories began to feud openly over their stance towards the European Union.

In 1994, after John Smith died of a heart attack, Tony Blair took over the leadership of the Labour Party. Embarking on a so-called party modernisation programme, he increased Labour's popularity and, on 1st May 1997, led the party back to power, after an 18-year absence, with a 179-seat majority.

**Dennis's parliamentary secretaries**

Dennis was able to step into the shoes of his friend and much-esteemed predecessor, Bob Edwards, inheriting his excellent secretarial arrangements. Dennis continued to employ the meticulous Hilary Davies as his secretary at Westminster, and the amiable workaholic, Jill Withers, as his secretary in the constituency office at Springvale in Wolverhampton.[11]

Hilary first met Dennis in June 1970, when she came up from London to Bilston to help Bob Edwards in his general election campaign, and Dennis was acting as Bob's election agent. They became firm friends, and during the next two election campaigns in 1974, and when she visited the constituency for surgeries, she stayed with Bob and Dennis at 'Ambleside', the house they shared in Bradley. She recalls going to bed, leaving them talking late into the night to work through their solutions to the world's problems. When Bob retired in 1987, she was happy to continue working for Dennis, as his successor.[12]

Jill was a member of the Springvale Ward Labour Party when she first met Dennis. When he was selected to fight Wolverhampton South East in 1987, he asked her to help him set up the constituency office.[13]

For eighteen years, the two secretaries worked as a team, one at each end of the telephone line, providing a seamless service. They organised Dennis's parliamentary papers, meetings and surgeries, and handled the constituents' correspondence and casework. Dennis pointed out that many of his clients were reluctant to commit to paper, often raising their concerns and asking for help in the pub and on the street. The scrappy notes that he left in the office had to be interpreted by his capable secretaries and followed up to provide satisfactory outcomes, a task they performed faultlessly.[14]

Jill told us that Dennis would never turn away anyone who asked for his help: "He held regular advice surgeries, but was frequently stopped in the local streets, or in a pub when he was enjoying a pint, or by British Rail staff, who got to know him on his regular journeys to London and back. He would write the name and address on the back of a receipt but, invariably, the detail of the case would be stored in his head. There would be numerous occasions when there would be a knock on his front door, sometimes as late as 10 o'clock at night. Whoever it was would be invited in, made welcome, and Dennis and Pat would listen to their problem for as long as it took, and then reassure them that they would do all they could to help."[15]

Hilary described how Dennis rarely used his office at Westminster, except as a storeroom for rapidly-accumulating piles of paper. "On most mornings, he would meet me instead in the Strangers' cafeteria to discuss the post, while he enjoyed his bacon sandwich. There were frequent interruptions while he greeted friends, or listened to the problems brought to him by various members of the canteen staff. He would also use these sessions in the cafeteria to dictate important letters."[16]

"He was not at all keen on the new technologies which were beginning to penetrate the Palace of Westminster. Following the 1997 election of the Labour government, Labour MPs were issued with pagers to ensure they remained 'on message'. Dennis did have a pager, but it was mostly to be found under the piles of paper on his desk and was then relegated to the bottom of the drawer in his desk. Despite his aversion to such devices, Dennis was more aware than most of what was happening in Westminster and the wider world. His well-honed methods of direct personal communication were far more effective!"[17]

**Nelson Mandela's 1996 speech to parliament**

When the black South African leader, Nelson Mandela, was released from prison, he made a series of visits to Europe famously meeting the prime minister, Mrs Thatcher, who had labelled the ANC a terrorist organisation. Much to her annoyance, he had expressed the opinion that Britain should start negotiating with the IRA. In 1993, he visited Britain, meeting the parents of the black teenager, Stephen Lawrence, who had been murdered by racist thugs on the streets of London. Invited to address both houses of parliament, he had declared that he was "deeply touched by the brutality of this murder even though it is commonplace in our country." Three years later, in 1996, thousands of people gathered to hear him speak in Trafalgar Square. Once again, on the 11th July 1996, he addressed the joint houses of parliament.

This occasion made a deep and lasting impression on Dennis, inspiring in later years his tireless work for the cause of international development and fair trade. He remembers Mandela's speech, not only for its call for reconciliation after the cruelty and humiliation of apartheid, but for its concise analysis of the social and economic challenges facing South Africa in the post-apartheid era.[18]

After Betty Boothroyd had welcomed the president of the South African Republic with a memorable speech of her own, Mandela spoke of 'the founding stones' of his new country: national reconciliation and unity, a democratic system that ensured that all citizens had an equal right and equal capacity to determine their future, and an end to the enormous race and gender disparities in wealth, income and opportunity, inherited from the past, which jeopardised the goals of national unity and reconciliation. Fully conscious of the immense disparities of wealth and income in the United Kingdom, Dennis not only identified with the South African 'founding stones', but thought they might well be used as the basis for the politics of a future Labour government!

**Gibraltar**

During the 1990s, Dennis took an interest in the debate over the sovereignty of Gibraltar and joined a parliamentary delegation to the Rock to learn the views of its people and politicians. He met Joe Bossano, the leader of the Gibraltar Socialist Labour Party and chief minister of Gibraltar until 1996. He became firm friends with Joe, whom he described as "a fine socialist".[19]

Dennis became convinced that the wishes of the Gibraltarians had to be taken into account in any discussion relating to the future of the British Overseas Territory. While the Labour government vacillated somewhat in its negotiations with Spain, Dennis went on Gibraltarian television to point out that the vast majority of the British people, including most ordinary Labour Party members, supported the Gibraltarians in their wish to remain British under the Crown. In the referendum held in Gibraltar in 2002, the proposal to share sovereignty with Spain was rejected by a majority of 98.97 per cent.

Dennis's brother Bert told us that when the Turner family had taken a holiday in Gibraltar, Dennis had been repeatedly recognised in the street, and congratulated for his stance with a shake of the hand.[20] Her Majesty's Government has since reaffirmed that it 'will never enter into arrangements under which the people of Gibraltar would pass under the sovereignty of another state against their freely and democratically expressed wishes'.

We were told by Dennis that the continued independence of Gibraltar under the Crown was a matter of great interest in the servicemen's clubs he visited, as many military personnel had passed through the base, or been stationed there.

Dennis went on asking questions about Gibraltar in the Lords. The last that we were able to locate related to the encroachment of the Spanish navy corvette 'Atalaya' in British Gibraltar territorial waters on 3 May 2011.[21]

**The All-Party Parliamentary Group for Further Education**

One of Dennis's first achievements at Westminster was to set up and serve for fifteen years as chair the All-Party Parliamentary Group for Further Education, now known as the All-Party Parliamentary Group for Further Education, Skills and Lifelong Learning. Its purpose is to promote and develop the interests of further education, adult learning and skills sectors and to advise government ministers on matters of concern to those sectors.[22] The group was first formed after the Conservative government passed the Further and Higher Education Act 1992.

Dennis had an abiding interest in further education, which he saw as an important means of saving young people from the evils of ignorance, unemployment and idleness and providing them with socially-beneficial values, training and education.

Cleverly conceived, the Further and Higher Education Act combined the popular and progressive measures of eradicating the higher education binary divide between the Universities Funding Council and the Polytechnics and Colleges Funding Council, with the more controversial decision to remove further education colleges and sixth-form colleges from local authority democratic control and to fund them through a Further Education Funding Council for England (FEFC). In the long run, the centralised and bureaucratic FEFC proved a mistake and was abolished after eight years by the Learning and Skills Act 2000.

From 1992 onwards, a forum was needed in which the interests of college governors and managers could be articulated. The new All-Party Parliamentary Group proved its worth in representing the further education interest, when James Paice, Parliamentary Under-secretary at the Department of Education and Employment, decided to remove £80 million from the further education budget half way through the financial year. The group began to play an increasingly important role in briefing ministers and senior education officials on the vicissitudes of further education colleges, with the not-for-profit Association of Colleges soon acting as its secretariat.

Christopher Walden, the director of public affairs and communications for the Association of Colleges recalled that Dennis was "a steadfast supporter of colleges" and his association "for the best part of 20 years, regularly chairing meetings, asking questions and raising our concerns quietly, but very effectively, with government...He persuaded the Chancellor, Gordon Brown, to come along to the group...producing a record attendance of MPs. Dennis would be as charming as ever in gently encouraging Mr Brown to go a step further in offering something to help the colleges with their work."[23]

## The All-Party Parliamentary Local Government Group

Dennis was also instrumental in convening the All-Party Parliamentary Local Government Group made up initially of the considerable number of MPs and Peers – 200 or more – who had once served as local councillors or council leaders. He was assisted in this task by David Clelland (MP for Tyne Bridge, 1995-2010) and Gerry Sutcliffe (MP for Bradford South 1994-current) former leaders respectively of Gateshead and Bradford Councils.[24]

Local government was experiencing intense scrutiny and criticism at the time and its voice was subdued. The group proved a rich source of hitherto untapped knowledge and networking power. Still extant, it seeks 'to promote the virtues of existing forms of first-tier local authorities, to inform policy making and initiatives affecting first-tier local authorities, and to stimulate debate on models of community governance'.[25]

**Membership of other all-party parliamentary groups**

In 2011, Gisela Stuart MP edited a comprehensive guide to parliament's 395 all-party groups (by our reckoning), supplying their purposes and their officers' names.[26] Dennis was not only active in the two groups mentioned above, but listed as a vice-chair of the Markets Group, which exists to promote and support traditional street and covered markets. He was secretary of the Group for Non-Profit Making Members' Clubs, aimed at supporting such clubs; joint chair, with Conservative, Andrew Rosindell, of the Greyhound Group, set up to raise parliamentary awareness of the greyhound industry; and joint vice-chair with Conservatives, Brian Binley and Karen Bradley, of the self-explanatory Save the Pub Group.[27] Dennis, for many years, was chair of the All-Party Racing and Bloodstock Industries Group, aimed at promoting horse racing, for which he had a special affection.[28] He was also active in all-party health interest groups, namely, those for Coeliac Disease and Dermatitis Herpetiformis, Diabetes, Lupus, and Stroke.[29]

He seems to have selected and joined these all-party groups for at least three reasons. In the cases of further education and local government, he clearly believed that the issues were important and needed to be promoted. Where markets, greyhounds, race horses, pubs, or working men's clubs were concerned, he possessed expert personal knowledge and an interest which he wanted to share. In regard to diabetes and stroke, of which he had personal experience, he shared an empathy and compassion with the victims of these, as well as of other diseases.[30]

*Dennis with his father, Bert Turner senior. Note Old Bert's cap which he was never seen without (courtesy of Barrie and Denise Nash).*

*Dennis and Pat with children, Jenny and Brendon, at the caravan in Tywyn, North Wales (courtesy of Pat Turner).*

*Dennis with his sister, Beryl, and brother, Bert (courtesy of Pat Turner).*

*A Labour night! In the pub, before the count for Wolverhampton Council elections. Dennis with Brenda and Ken Purchase (courtesy of Ken Purchase).*

*A graduation ceremony at Bilston Community College, with Dennis seated next to the Principal, Ivor Keith Wymer.*

Norman Davies, Dennis Turner, Neil Kinnock and Phil Bateman campaigning outside the Grand Theatre, Wolverhampton, in the run-up to the 1987 General Election.

Dennis Turner meeting Cherie Blair at Wolverhampton train station on her visit to Wolverhampton (courtesy of the Express & Star).

Dennis receiving the freedom of the City of Wolverhampton, accompanied by his family: wife, Pat, and children Brendon and Jenny, December 2006 (courtesy of the Express and Star).

*The residents of Bradley raise funds for charity by following 'the yellow-brick road'. The Turner brothers, Dr Lal, and Frank Venton are pictured alongside other prominent Bradleyites (courtesy of the Express and Star).*

*Dennis in ermine at his investiture in the House of Lords, accompanied by daughter, Jenny, wife, Pat, and son, Brendon (courtesy of the Express & Star).*

*Dennis with a bottle of Dennis beer, brewed to commemorate the campaign for the full pint and presented to Dennis by CAMRA and Banks's (courtesy of the Express & Star).*

*Dennis with parliamentary colleagues
(courtesy of the Express & Star).*

*The opening of the Black Country Route, left to right,
Trudy Bowen, Wolverhampton Mayor, Neil Kinnock,
Labour Party leader, Dennis Turner, and Norman
Davies, Leader of the Wolverhampton Labour Group
and Council (courtesy of the Express & Star).*

*Dennis, with his wife Pat at his side, celebrates his election to parliament in 1987 (courtesy of the Express & Star).*

*Dennis with the Springvale co-operators. The Springvale Sports and Social Club was set up in 1981 by ten redundant steel workers pooling their redundancy money.*

*Dennis, with Pat, his wife (courtesy of Pat Turner).*

*Dennis with his children, Jenny and Brendon (courtesy of Pat Turner).*

*Dennis and Sir Keith Joseph exchanging words outside the Edgbaston Conservative Rooms on 22 February 1980 during the National Steel Strike (courtesy of Bert Turner).*

*Dennis as a young man addressing the Iron and Steel Trades Confederation Delegate Conference. Prince Charles, to the left of the platform party, listens intently (courtesy of Bert Turner).*

*The Swan public house at the end of Bilston High Street, one of Dennis's favourite watering holes.*

*Bilston sculpture 'Women's work', better known as 'Anvil Annie', by Rose Garrard, unveiled by Clare Short, Secretary of State for International Development, May 1998.*

*Lord Street, Bradley, Bilston, where Dennis lived for much of his life.*

*The entrance to St Martin's built in 1900, where Dennis attended church and primary school. The church building itself has since been demolished following a fire.*

*The council house in Powell Place, Bradley, Bilston (long since refurbished) in which the Turner family was rehoused in 1949.*

*A view of the Bilston steel works, about 1968.*

*The Bradley Senior Citizens Centre opened in 1971 by Councillor Dennis Turner on behalf of the Bradley Trust Committee.*

*A protest held outside Enoch Powell's constituency office on the Tettenhall Road, Wolverhampton South West, following his 'river of blood' speech on the 20 April 1968.*

*Laying the foundation stone for the New Cross Hospital Heart and Lung Centre, 2003, right to left, Dennis Turner, Ken Purchase, Alan Milburn and Professor Mel Chevannes, Royal Wolverhampton Hospital Trust chair.*

# Chapter 11

## International development and fair trade

### From whipping to catering

While in opposition, Dennis was made the Labour whip for the 73 Labour Members of Parliament in the West Midlands – one of the largest groups of Labour MPs in the post-1992 parliament. He was also appointed to be Labour whip for education under two shadow Secretaries of State for Education: Ann Taylor (from 1992 to 1994) (now Baroness Taylor of Bolton) and David Blunkett (from 1994, becoming Secretary of State for Education and Employment until 1997).[1]

The political analyst, Dennis Kavanagh, described Dennis's approach as a whip to be along the lines: "'If it's not too much trouble, do you think you could possibly…?' With an avuncular manner, shaking hands and draping an arm around the shoulder of MPs, he was effective." [2]

After the Labour landslide victory of 1997, however, such was the pressure from senior Labour MPs to find places for those loyal to them, that Dennis, who was never a camp follower, found himself squeezed out of the government whips' office. By way of a consolation prize, he was invited by Tony Blair to become chair of the Commons Catering Committee which oversaw the catering and retail services, including bars, restaurants and cafeteria.[3]

This inspired appointment drew on Dennis's unique knowledge of catering and bars, acquired originally as chair of the aforementioned Springvale Social Club Cooperative. It also brought with it the right to sit on the Commons Liaison Committee, made up of the chairmen of all the other select committees, brought together to consider select committees' work and to decide on which of their reports should be debated in the House.[4]

One of Dennis's successes was to have Banks's mild, brewed in Wolverhampton, and served at the counter of the Stranger's Bar.[5] During the week, homesick West Midlands MPs relished the amazing prospect of having such a pint pulled in the House. Another was the introduction of Fair Trade goods explained in more detail below. One of Dennis's major achievements was to establish the Jubilee Café, which extended the Palace of Westminster's corporate catering capacity to accommodate substantial parties of visitors.[6] Prior to the opening of this facility, the Commons could take only very small groups at a time.

In one month alone, Dennis organised day visits from Wolverhampton to the House for 1,000 old-age pensioners in parties of 250 at a time, accommodated in five coaches. The Wolverhampton pensioners not only visited parliament, but travelled from the Westminster Pier down the Thames to visit the Tower of London before catching the coach home.[7]

In 2005, when Dennis left the Commons, the Catering Committee, along with four other former domestic committees, was absorbed under a newly-formed Administration Committee.

**Dennis becomes a parliamentary private secretary**

Clare Short was elected Labour MP for Birmingham Ladywood, in 1983, and like Dennis, represented the constituency where she had grown up, until she chose to leave parliament in 2010. During the 1990s, when Labour was in opposition, she joined the Labour front bench, becoming, in turn, shadow minister for women, shadow transport secretary, and then being given the overseas development portfolio.

When Labour took power after the 1997 general election, Tony Blair gave the Overseas Development Administration, then in the Foreign Office, full departmental status, as the Department of International Development, and Clare was made the first-ever Secretary of State for International Development, with a seat in the cabinet.

Clare asked Dennis, a fellow West Midlands MP, to become her parliamentary private secretary (PPS).[8] (A PPS is an unpaid position designated by a senior minister, with the prime minister's approval, to act as a contact in the Commons and, if necessary, as a stand-in.)

## Department for International Development

Clare's first task, ably assisted by Dennis, was to plan, organise, and set up the new department, which involved the transfer of staff from the Foreign Office into a new office in Victoria Street, Westminster, London, and the adoption of an entirely new way of thinking about international development, untainted by short-term commercial interests.

This involved adopting a set of 'millennium development goals' – to eradicate extreme poverty and hunger, achieve universal primary education, promote gender equality and empower women, reduce child morality, improve maternal health, combat HIV and AIDS, malaria and other diseases, ensure environmental sustainability, and develop global partnerships (this last referring to action necessary to deal with the debt burden of developing countries). The 'millennium goals' were identified in consultation with aid agencies and the churches and written into the constitution of the new department.

Dennis remembered this as a wonderful period in which Clare provided outstanding leadership, steering Britain away from the unsavoury policies of the former Conservative government. The most notorious instance, of course, was that of the Pergau dam and power station in Malaysia, which had been constructed with British taxpayers' money on the insistence of Mrs Thatcher, in order to secure a major arms deal.

## Monserrat incident

Clare Short retained her position as Secretary of State for International Development, with Dennis as her PPS, throughout the Labour government's first term and beyond the general election of 2001, into the second. Clare's leadership was not without incident.

In 1995, the Soufriere volcano on Monserrat, one of Britain's overseas territories in the Caribbean, erupted, forcing two-thirds of the island's population to flee. In 1997, there were further explosions, lava flows, and ash clouds, killing 19 people. The Monserratians called upon the British government to provide them with more assistance, a request which is said to have been met by Clare with the remark, "they will be asking for golden elephants next", and a refusal to visit the island. This political blunder, which caused great offence to the islanders, was compensated for when, in 1998, Clare arranged for the people of Monserrat to be granted full residency rights in the United Kingdom.

## Zimbabwe

In November 1997, Clare declined to fund land reform in Zimbabwe, unless it was coupled to a poverty eradication programme, incurring the wrath of Robert Mugabe and his government, who argued that British aid had been promised in the Lancaster House Agreement of 1979.

## Land mines

In 1997, Clare signed the Ottawa Convention, committing Britain to a ban on the production, handling, and use of land mines. Another of Clare and Dennis's notable achievements was to get the International Development Act, 17 June 2002, onto the statute book. It ensured that poverty reduction was at the centre of the DfID's work and it finally outlawed the abuse of tied aid – endemic to previous administrations.

## Iraq

In March 2003, in the run-up to the second Iraq war, Clare began openly to disagree with Tony Blair, calling him "reckless", for leading Britain to war without a United Nations mandate. As it became clear that the country was going to war, Clare did in fact resign, but was prevailed upon by colleagues, including Dennis, to withdraw her resignation on the promise that she and the DfID would have a vital role to play in providing humanitarian assistance after the conflict.[9] She remained in the cabinet, voting in the Commons, together with Dennis, to back the 2003 Iraq war.

In pursuit of the essential humanitarian role suggested to her by Tony Blair, she and Dennis flew to America to hold discussions at the United Nations, the World Bank, International Monetary Fund, and the US State Department, only to realise that the George W Bush administration, and Donald Rumsfeld, the US Secretary of Defence, were not in the slightest bit interested in what they had to say.[10] Clare resigned her ministerial position on 12 May 2003, bringing Dennis's six-year career as a parliamentary private secretary to an end. His friend and fellow Wolverhampton MP, Ken Purchase, who for six years had served as PPS to Robin Cook, met a similar fate when Cook, too, resigned from the cabinet over the Iraq war.

In 2014, Clare Short came to Dennis's funeral, telling the press that "the stories everyone has told of his incredible friendliness are true. Inside, there were steely principles, but he was such a lovable person, and there aren't many like him."[11] Dennis's close friendship with Clare had long since cooled, following her resignation of the Labour whip in October 2006, after declaring that she would campaign for a hung parliament and was profoundly ashamed of the Labour Party.

**Fair trade**

As the driving political force at the newly-instituted Department for International Development, Clare and Dennis continued to pursue a course dear to their hearts – a commitment to the fair-trade movement.[12] The first attempts at trading fairly with developing countries were initiated by non-governmental organisations (NGOs), including religious groups, in the 1940s and 1950s. In those days, 'fair trade' referred to the importation of handicrafts from developing countries which were then sold at fairs and church fetes.

The current fair-trade movement emerged in the 1960s as a critique of, and challenge to the unfettered capitalist business deals and multi-national corporate market dominance which left poor countries at a distinct economic disadvantage, and which was leading to increased impoverishment and debt.

## 'Helping by selling'

In 1995, Oxfam launched its 'Helping by Selling' campaign, which sold imported handicrafts in its shops and by mail-order. By the 1970s, activists were exploring new markets for products, such as coffee from Nicaragua or Angola, then excluded for political reasons from trading internationally.

In the 1990s, handicrafts dominated fair-trade outlets but, by 2002, two-thirds of sales value came from agricultural goods, such as tea, coffee, dried fruit, cocoa, sugar, fruit juice, rice, spices, and nuts. Fair-trade products really took off with the introduction of fair-trade certification. The certification aimed to guarantee not only fair prices, but the principle of ethical purchasing, for example, an assurance that goods had not been produced with child or slave labour, that they came from a safe workplace, and that the workforce had the freedom to join trade unions. Currently, the United Kingdom is thought to have the most dynamic fair-trade market in the world, with the widest range of products and the most diverse range of companies.

## Fairtrade at DfID and the House of Commons

At the DfID, Clare and Dennis ensured that the government remained committed to fair and ethical trade, and began the process of providing development grants to the Fairtrade Foundation and other projects involving fair trade. Clare insisted that all DfID hospitality tea and coffee should be Fairtrade, a policy that has since been extended to include most of the snacks on sale in the DfID's cafeteria and other sales outlets. As chair of the committee in charge of the House of Commons bars, restaurants and cafeteria, Dennis presided over the introduction in November 1997 of Fairtrade coffee, making the House of Commons the first major British public institution to do so.

## Wolverhampton, a Fairtrade city

In 2000, Dennis asked Clare, as Secretary of State for International Development, to launch a conference on fair trade in Wolverhampton. Following the event, a working party was set up under Dennis's chairmanship to establish the Wolverhampton Fairtrade Partnership. The partnership then persuaded Wolverhampton City Council to adopt Fairtrade status and become a Fairtrade City, a resolution agreed at full council in 2004.

Valerie Amos, Labour life peer (who was appointed Secretary of State for International Development following Clare's resignation in 2003) came to launch the city's initiative. With its tenth anniversary due in 2014, Dennis chaired the Wolverhampton Fairtrade Partnership from the start.

When news of Dennis's serious illness began to circulate in January 2014, Barbara Gwinnett, the secretary of the Wolverhampton Fairtrade Partnership, wrote to Dennis, enclosing a note from her young grandson, which cheered him no end. It read: 'I hope you are getting better. Granny has told me you have been in hospital and that is sad. I loved going to London and meeting you and seeing the House of Lords. If you get better, maybe we could come again and have some curly chips. Lots of love, Alfie.'[13]

## Indian Ocean tsunami

Dennis's longstanding commitment to the cause of international development and aid is illustrated by the delightful picture of him participating in a Bradley event to raise money for the victims of the Indian Ocean tsunami of December 2004. The good people of Bradley, including Dennis, Brother Bert Turner, 87-year-old Frank Venton, and local GP, Dr Lal, can be seen holding arms and doing a Wizard-of-Oz-style jig along an imaginary 'yellow-brick road', on a walk which eventually raised £30,000 for the Disaster Emergency Committee Appeal. Fundraising for a far-away cause, such as this, contrasted markedly with a Bilston Christmas charity collection some 35 years previously, in which the organisers insisted on stipulating that every penny raised would be spent exclusively on the needy of Bilston.

Dennis was determined to support charitable causes at local, national and international levels, and he and Patty maintained this principle in making their own personal donations. Besides supporting emergency appeals, such as the Pakistani earthquake disaster and East African famine relief, they particularly favoured collections on behalf of disabled and disadvantaged children, people with special needs, and the elderly and infirm. They gave generously to the Salvation Army, the NSPCC, and Age UK, and were members of the UK United Nations Organisation, Oxfam, and Amnesty.[14]

## Regional government

Dennis and David Clelland were strongly in favour of regional government and helped set up the Regional Government Group in parliament, of which David was secretary, under the chairmanship of Richard Caborn. In November 2004, the first referendum for a regional assembly, as part of Labour's devolution process, was held in the North East, where David had his constituency. The proposal was rejected by 77.9 per cent of the electorate on a turnout of 49 per cent. David told us that both he and Dennis remained convinced that, with the increasing gravitational pull of London and the South East, devolution to the regions was a progressive idea whose time had yet to come.[15]

## Wolverhampton Heart and Lung Centre

Dennis retained a primary interest in the health and wellbeing of his constituents and the people of Wolverhampton and used his position in parliament to lobby relentlessly on their behalf. Under a Labour government, he was often spectacularly successful in attracting projects and resources to the city.

When Alan Milburn took over from Frank Dobson as Secretary of State for Health from 1999, Dennis, together with Wolverhampton's two other MPs, Ken Purchase and Jenny Jones, met with the new minister to make the case for a new cardio-thoracic facility to be situated in the west of the West Midlands conurbation. At the time, heart patients in the town had to travel as far as Walsgrave Hospital in Coventry for treatment.[16] The research evidence certainly supported the case for developing a service such as this at the Royal Wolverhampton Hospitals NHS Trust at New Cross.

The Wolverhampton MPs must have been persuasive, for shortly afterwards, a much-needed £44 million regional cardiac and cardiology centre was approved for the New Cross site. Construction began in October 2002 and was completed on time in December 2004. Alan Milburn, the Secretary of State for Health, came to Wolverhampton for the topping-out ceremony in January 2003. He was pictured in a hard hat, along with the trust chair, Mel Chevannes, and MPs, Dennis and Ken Purchase. Prior to the centre coming into service, local patients were required to wait for up to eighteen months for treatment at other West Midlands hospitals.[17]

The centre was described at its opening as costing £60 million, and having seven wards, four operating theatres, two catheterisation suites, a critical care unit and an out-patient department, dedicated to providing cardiac and thoracic surgery, secondary and tertiary cardiology, rehabilitation, clerical measurement and day procedures. Currently, the Heart and Lung Centre, as it is now called, averages 72 heart operations per month, or 864 per year.

Without the case for the centre, ably advanced by Professor Mel Chevannes, chair of the hospital trust and Dennis's friend, and the persistent and vigorous lobbying of Wolverhampton MPs, local people, in all likelihood, would still be experiencing delays and travelling long distances for operations, with attendant illness, pain, and unnecessary loss of life.

**Party loyalty**

Dennis was not without controversy in the policies and causes he espoused in parliament. Against his better judgment, he voted in favour of the deployment of the armed forces in Afghanistan and the invasion of Iraq in 2003. He voted with gritted teeth for the rise in university tuition fees, the school academy programme, and foundation hospitals.

This voting record, for which, in hindsight, he expressed some regret, can only be understood in the context of his background in the trade union movement, his belief in the importance of party loyalty, discipline, and solidarity, and his one-time position as a Labour whip. He felt obliged to support the party line in the interests of the bigger picture, although his heart was not always in the policy being pursued, particularly as the party swung to the right under Tony Blair. He never accepted the logic of privatisation and was fearful of the effects of the application of the purchaser/provider model to NHS and local government services, particularly in regard to residential provision for the sick and older people.

Pat McFadden, MP for Wolverhampton South East from 2005, summed up Dennis's political track record in the following way: "First and foremost, he was a strong and loyal supporter of the Labour government. He was aware of the damage the Tory years had done to his constituency, and appreciated the difference a Labour government could make. He was uncomfortable with some of the New Labour changes, especially in the provision of public services, such as health and education, but could never bring himself to go into opposition mode against his very own government. This may have been because he'd served in the whip's office, but I think a more convincing explanation lay in his unshakeable belief that although you might disagree with a particular policy, in the final analysis, it was still your government and you had to stick together."[18]

Roger Lawrence, Wolverhampton council leader, made the same point: "Dennis was clearly uneasy with some of the direction of New Labour, but he was essentially a tribal loyalist, and expressed dissent softly and in sadness, rather than in anger."[19]

# Chapter 12

## Friends in high places

### Dennis's friends in parliament

Prior to and in the course of his parliamentary career, Dennis made a number of long-lasting friendships and alliances based on the sharing of common political values and experience, comradeship, and loyalty. Among his many dear friends were, in alphabetical order, David Blunkett, Betty Bothroyd, David Clelland, John Evans, Bruce Grocott, Ken Purchase, Peter Snape and Ann Taylor. Dennis was acutely aware that as in football, it required disciplined team building, comradeship, and unselfish cooperation to achieve one's political goal.

### David Blunkett

David Blunkett, the MP for Sheffield Brightside, entered parliament in 1987, at the same time as Dennis. Like Dennis who had been elected to Wolverhampton Council in 1966 at the age of 23, David had become the youngest councillor on Sheffield City Council, winning his seat in 1970 when he was just 22. Both had served for long periods in local government, Dennis from 1966 to 1986, and David from 1970 to 1988. Both came from poor working-class backgrounds and had been brought up in harsh circumstances, made far more severe for David because he had been blind from birth.

David's subsequent parliamentary career had been meteoric. Following Labour's victory in 1997, he had become, in turn, Secretary of State for Education, Home Secretary, and Work and Pensions Secretary, but had on occasion, found himself personally vulnerable and in need of a helping hand, which Dennis, as always, had been only too willing to offer.

Dennis recalled with glee the occasion in March 1999 when David's guide dog, Lucy, vomited on the floor of the House during a speech by David

Willetts, the Shadow Secretary of State for Education, a spontaneous canine commentary, it was said, on Tory education policy. Dennis, in gratitude, assisted in the clean up – off the floor!

## Betty Boothroyd

Betty Boothroyd was the West Midlands MP who represented West Bromwich from 1973 to 2000. She became Deputy Speaker of the House of Commons in 1987 and was elected Speaker in 1992, the first woman to hold the position, serving until October 2000. In 2001, she was made a life peer, with the title Baroness Boothroyd of Sandwell.

Like Dennis, she followed football, but supported a rival team: West Bromwich Albion. Nevertheless, she and Dennis remained firm friends. Dennis recalled how he became known for standing next to her throne in the Commons, where they would chat together informally. They both shared an asthmatic condition, and on one occasion, Dennis persuaded Betty to take one of his ventolin tablets, causing her to shake - an experience she chose not to repeat.

## David Clelland

Another of Dennis's friends was the working-class Labour MP, David Clelland. Born in Gateshead, he attended the local Kelvin Grove Boys School and Gateshead and Hebburn Technical College, before working as an electrical fitter to Reyrolle in Hebburn for 22 years. Like Dennis, he followed the local council route into politics: he was elected to Gateshead Borough Council in 1972 and became Labour leader in 1984. In 1985, he was selected to fight the Tyne Bridge by-election, a seat he won and held until standing down in 2010. Like Dennis, he served as a Labour Party whip in opposition, but became an assistant government whip following the 1997 General Election. In common with Dennis, he has a fine voice and goes to the dogs, on the subject of which he is so knowledgeable that, in 2002, Richard Caborn, the Minister of Sport, sought his advice on greyhound racing.

Dennis and David formed the backbone of an MPs' male voice choir which met in the Strangers' Bar in the course of late-night sittings.[1] Dennis took the role of conductor of the chorus, but members also gave voice to their own favourite solos. Dennis remembers, in particular, a rendering of 'Singing in the rain', in which George Foulkes, yet another singing MP - and an aspiring Gene Kelly - equipped with umbrella, jumped from stool to stool, while the soda siphon on the bar was used to provide the necessary precipitation.[2]

David Clelland and Dennis used to organise a social event for Labour MPs which came to be known as 'the works outing'. Held annually in the Albert on Victoria Street, it aimed to remind them of their fundamental working-class socialist roots. The entertainment included the singing of socialist anthems and ditties, at which David and Dennis were well versed. Attended by an average of 120 MPs, the works outings began in 1988 and were held annually over a period of 20 years, until Dennis retired. In 2012, the outing was revived and David Watts, the new chair of the parliamentary Labour Party used the occasion to acknowledge David and Dennis's contributions to the event by asking Ed Milliband to sign and present them with commemorative photographs.[3]

In addition to their common interests in singing, the performance arts, and greyhound racing, David and Dennis were both enthusiastic supporters of the working men's clubs movement and the CIU. After David's retirement from parliament in 2010, Dennis persuaded the CIU executive to retain his involvement by making him their unpaid parliamentary advisor. David continues to support the All-Party Parliamentary Group for Non-Profit Making Members' Clubs.[4]

### John Evans

The Labour MP, John Evans, also came from a solid working-class background, having been a shipyard worker and trade unionist. He was elected to parliament in 1974 for the Newton constituency, a seat which he kept until it was abolished at the 1983 election. John was then elected to the new St Helens North constituency, which took in part of the same area.

Dennis and John shared a common experience of representing constituencies desperate for inward investment, industrial renewal, and job creation. John stood down in 1997 and was made a life peer with the title Baron Evans of Parkside of St Helens in the County of Merseyside. John and Dennis were colleagues in both the Commons and the Lords.

## Bruce Grocott

Dennis's colleague and confidant, Bruce Grocott worked in the West Midlands for many years as a lecturer at Birmingham Polytechnic and later at North Staffordshire Polytechnic. He was active in his local Labour Party branch, serving for a while on Bromsgrove District Council. He first entered parliament in 1974 as the member for Lichfield and Tamworth, but lost his seat in 1979. He joined Central Television as a producer and presenter, on one occasion making a programme sympathetic to the cause of the Bilston steel workers. He was re-elected for the Wrekin constituency in 1987, at the same time that Dennis entered parliament. Shortly afterwards, Bruce was made deputy shadow leader of the House, and under John Smith, became Labour spokesman on foreign affairs.[5]

Like Dennis, he served as a parliamentary private secretary but, in Bruce's case, to Tony Blair, the prime minister, for whom he worked from 1994 to the general election in 2001. He chose not to stand again in 2001, but returned to Westminster as a life peer under the title Baron Grocott of Telford. He served as government Chief Whip in the Lords from 2002 to 2008.

Bruce, who had sat with Dennis in the Commons and Lords, commented without prompting on his friend's great loyalty and authenticity: "There is nothing false or manufactured about him. His loyalties are for life and unshakeable – to his family, to his friends, to his community, to his trade union, and to the Labour Party."[6]

In 2013, as Lord Grocott, Bruce was elected to be chancellor of the University of Leicester, his old alma mater. Bruce has been most helpful in identifying what he felt were Dennis's significant contributions to the Commons and Lords and asking other colleagues to write appreciations. Supportive of the Turner family to the last, he was invited to speak at Dennis's funeral.

## Ken Purchase

Ken Purchase and Dennis were brought up in Wolverhampton and worked in local industry, Ken as an apprentice toolmaker in a foundry and tool room machinist in the car industry, Dennis as a stocktaker and transport controller at the steel works. Both were members of the Young Socialists and stood in local ward elections for Wolverhampton Council, Ken serving from 1970 to 1990, and Dennis from 1966 to 1986. Ken was elected in 1992 as MP for Wolverhampton North East (next to the South East constituency), retaining the seat until he stood down in 2010. Both Ken and Dennis were Co-operative Party MPs and shared a house together when they stayed in London. As one of Dennis's oldest political colleagues, Ken, too, was asked to address the congregation at Dennis's funeral.

## Peter Snape

Another of Dennis's mates was Peter Snape. Like Dennis, he has a working-class background, starting his career as a railway clerk and guard in the Stockport area. He served as MP for West Bromwich East for 27 years, from 1974 to 2001, joining the Lords in 2004, after a break from parliament of three years. Edwina Curry, the Conservative MP, became so infuriated with Peter after a television debate that she famously poured a glass of orange juice over him.

## Ann Taylor

Ann Taylor was the MP for Bolton West from 1974 until 1983, when she lost her seat, and then for Dewsbury from 1987 to 2005. She held a number of front-bench roles, more recently from 1994 to 1998, as shadow leader of the House of Commons and, from 1998 to 2001, as the government's Chief

Whip. In common with Dennis, she stepped down from the Commons at the 2005 general election and was given a life peerage as Baroness Taylor of Bolton.

Dennis was keen for us to mention still more of his parliamentary colleagues and acquaintances but, at this point, we used our editorial prerogative to draw this chapter to a close.

# Chapter 13

## Remoulded nearer to the heart's desire

### Dennis's Black Country industrial roots

Dennis was immensely proud of Bradley, his place of birth in the former Black Country Borough of Bilston. In his first address to the House of Lords, he explained in some detail why he had chosen the territorial title of 'Bilston':

"The title of Bilston is taken from my Black Country town and birthplace. It is a former borough with over 1,000 years of history; an industrial town forged out of the white heat of the industrial revolution; a place of little sunshine, where the gin pits, puddling furnaces and fiery holes produced the black and grey smoke that darkened the skies and pervaded the landscape. That was the era of John 'Iron Mad' Wilkinson, who built, in Bradley, Bilston, the first furnace for making iron for commercial production of iron household utensils which were soon to be marketed around the world. It was John Wilkinson who launched the first iron boat on the local canal and who built his own iron coffin."[1]

He went on to describe the historical development of Bilston:

"This was a landscape rich in coal, iron ore and limestone, all the ingredients to make Bilston an early industrial boom-town, where waves of migration from Wales, Scotland, Ireland and neighbouring counties changed a quiet hamlet of hundreds into a community of thousands of workers and their families, who, by their industrial knowledge, strength and resilience, created the vibrant economy by which the Black Country became known as the 'workshop of the world'. Today, with the enrichment of our cultural and religious diversity from the new Commonwealth and other parts of the world, Bilston is still a friendly manufacturing, metal-bashing town, with a strong identity and pride."[2]

## Safeguarding the Bilston heritage

With the formation in 1966 of a greater Wolverhampton, the previous local government administrators, institutions and property of Bilston, Tettenhall and Wednesfield came under the control of Wolverhampton Borough Council and, in the formation of the new corporate entity, were inevitably subsumed and rationalised.

Councillors representing wards of the old Bilston soon came to recognise the that the merger had been a mixed blessing, and posed a threat to beloved local landmarks such as the former town hall, the market, the library and the museum and art gallery. They were now faced with the additional challenge of protecting and defending the social and economic fabric of the former borough in the face of the centrifuge of power which, with predictable inevitability, was beginning to concentrate resources at the centre of Wolverhampton.

For Dennis, this was not merely a matter of personal nostalgia, but a serious economic issue. Services were being siphoned away from the poorer margins of the town, such as Bradley, towards the more affluent centre, a couple of bus rides away.[3]

With this insight, Dennis always made sure that, on his watch, the people of Bilston received their fair share of the various funds available for urban renewal and development. His success can be judged on the existence to this day of a vibrant shopping area, with its own bustling high street, market and tram and bus station, situated to the south east of Wolverhampton City Centre. Contemporary Bilston has maintained a distinctive identity, quite unlike anywhere else in the borough, thanks to the efforts, made over many years, of its local ward councillors, led by Dennis Turner as Bilston's councillor, MP, and Lord, in league with his older brother, Councillor Thomas Herbert (Bert) Turner.[4]

## Return of the Bilston enamels

One matter that for many years had rankled with Bilston residents was the decision to downgrade the Bilston Art Gallery and Museum in Brueton House on Mount Pleasant and remove its display of local artefacts – including a wonderful collection of Bilston enamel boxes – to more secure venues in Wolverhampton. The campaign to have these treasures returned to Bilston was waged more tenaciously and with greater indignation than the Greek government's demand for the return of the Elgin Marbles.

In 1999, with the help of a National Lottery grant, the Bilston Craft Gallery was refurbished with modern security arrangements and, in 2004, a 'Craftsense' exhibition was opened, to display Bilston crafts from the 1700s onwards. It featured the largest collection of Bilston enamels in the country.[5]

When Bert and Kath Turner served as the Mayor and Mayoress of Wolverhampton for 2011 to 2012, they noticed the mayoral chains of office and ceremonial mace of the former Borough of Bilston on display in the cabinets lining the mayor's parlour in the Civic Centre. There and then, Bert and Kath resolved to have the Bilston mayoral regalia returned to Bilston.[6] The superb silver chains, pendants, and mace, adorned, in the finest taste, with 1930s Bilston enamel heraldic figures and emblems, are now on display in the craft gallery, along with a magnificent casket containing the scroll of the borough's freedom, donated by James Luther Greenway, a leading Bilston industrialist.[7]

## Modern Bilston

Nowhere is the Turners' contribution more obvious, however, than in the area on either side of Bilston High Street, Church Street, and the Black Country Route. Here can be found the refurbished Bilston town hall, a new police station, the seven-stand bus station, the new Midland Metro tramline to Birmingham and tram station, the indoor market, a handsome brick-built job centre, Morrisons and Lidl supermarkets, the recently-completed South

Wolverhampton and Bilston Academy, and the state-of-the-art Bert Williams Leisure Centre which, taken together with the Black Country Route itself, provide concrete evidence of substantial inward investment. As was only to be expected, the leisure centre was opened to the public on the 3rd December 2011 by the mayor of Wolverhampton, Bert Turner, and Bert Williams, MBE.

But the modern Bilston townscape possesses a distinctive appearance extending far beyond these impressive structures. The town is uniquely endowed with its own magnificent display of street sculpture and furniture which, unlike so many modern public works of art, has been specially designed and erected with a single important shared purpose: to instil in Bilstonians a sense of pride in their 250-year heritage of coal, iron and steel production and the essential role played by this small Black Country town in the great industrial revolution.

### The Bilston sculpture park

At one end of the High Street in front of the Horse and Jockey public house is a four-meter bronze figure of a woman entitled 'women's work', but known locally as 'Anvil Annie', by the Malvern sculptor, Rose Garrard. It commemorates women workers in the local coal and iron industries of the 19th century. On closer inspection, the woman's body comprises a small anvil for her head, tongs for her forearms, flat irons for feet, and stacked iron cooking pots for legs. Fused into her apron are nails and chain links, and on her back, supported by a head belt, is a heavy burden of coal lumps gleaned, we are told, from a slag heap near the pit head.

The sculpture was commissioned by Wolverhampton Borough Council, sponsored by Tarmac and, at Dennis's request, unveiled by Clare Short in May 1998, when she was Secretary of State for International Development, and he was her PPS.[8]

Nearby, between High Street and Church Street, on the parapet of the bridge spanning the Midland Metro tramway is another interesting sculpture, by artist Bettina Furnée, consisting of a frieze of great metal slabs, reminiscent of the 19th century cast-iron grave stones set into the pavement in front of St Leonard's church. Each is inscribed with the recollections of Bilston's older citizens – capturing, in cast metal, the oral history of the place, of its commerce and industry. One slab reads:

You could have mild
and you could have bitter
Even if it was
Pitchblack with fog
Town used to be packed
full every night
There were so many
on either side
of the road


Another:

Bilston Steel Works was
the heart of the area
The furnaces there
made anything
from anything
When the Steel Works closed
Probably 2500 jobs went
Open the doors!
The blast furnace blow out
The melting shop

Yet another:

THE FURNACE THAT CRIPPLED ME

And another:

## THE SKY LIT
## UP IN A
## BIG BURST
## OF RED GLOW

Bilston Job Centre on the corner of the High Street and Smith Street is said to be the most attractive place to search for work in the Black Country, if not the UK, or quite possibly the world. Above its gabled entrance, a large brick ceramic mural in bas-relief, possibly 3x3 meters, by sculptor John McKenna, depicts two steel workers pouring molten metal into moulds, along with an assortment of chains, cogs, pulleys and bars. We asked Dennis how Bilston had managed to acquire such a building gem, only to be told that it was high time that we realised that the unemployed of Bilston deserved only the best![9] As explained in Chapter 5, the building was opened in 1996 by Bert Williams, the former England goalie.

A box-like tower constructed of steel columns at the side of the Black Country Route marks the site of a large Morrison's supermarket. This prominent structure, capped with a pyramidal roof, is hung on three sides with translucent panels decorated with blue and orange-coloured silhouettes depicting various local industrial processes, for example, three men with tongs carrying an ingot of steel.

Placed along the raised pathway situated next to the route and the market car park, are a further series of heavy steel sculptures reflecting the mass and forms of the machinery and tools associated with iron and steel production, and variously entitled 'Breadwinner', 'Tools of the trade', 'Glory Hole' and 'Enshrined Pressure'. Even the brickwork below the footbridge spanning the route was specially designed by artist, Jane Kelly, to evoke the industrial past.

On the traffic island at the junction of the High Street and Millfields Road is our favourite Bilston sculpture, unimaginatively titled 'three columns', but what we have come to call 'iron henge', a set of three 10-meter-high rusty-brown steel monoliths by sculptor, Miles Davies. 'Iron henge' was commissioned by Wolverhampton Borough Council and installed in June 1996, but was, we recall, criticised at the time for its rust-bucket appearance, suggesting industrial decay rather than renewal.

On the neighbouring Coseley Road roundabout in front of the fire station is 'Beth's arch', another impressive 8-meter metal structure, showing a male and a female figure stretching upwards to form a bridge, the male rising from the flames of a furnace, the female emerging from a lumpy formation of coal and iron ore. The sculptor was Sarah Tombs and the work was commissioned once more by the Wolverhampton Borough Council and installed in July 1996.

A further impressive monument to the industrial past is Robin Erskine's stainless steel 'Roll Down', situated in Springvale Avenue near to the traffic island adjacent to Halfords, and commissioned by Blue Lamp Business Parks Ltd. Dennis was invited to unveil it on the 19th October 1994. It stands on the site of the Springvale Works and symbolises an ingot of white-hot steel being squeezed through a rolling mill, significantly the very same process that Dennis's father, Bert, used to perform at the plant.

Individually, none of these sculptures is sufficient to bestow on Bilston a distinctive identity but, when viewed collectively, within the overall framework imposed by the ubiquitous street furniture, they stake out the boundaries of the bailey of Bilston as effectively as the walls of a mediaeval city. Defending the heartland of the High Street are the metal railings and solid steel archways and lintels which mark the entries to folds and alleyways. Sturdy steel benches, jumbo wrought-iron sofas with sun motifs, and columns capped with sheet metal crests blazoned with badges, complete this magnificent pageantry.

## The value of community

This new phoenix-like Bilston is, in reality, the lifetime work of one man, transfixed by the revelation that the key to his neighbourhood's future economic prosperity lay in being fiercely proud of one's working-class roots and industrial heritage, and in retaining and valuing one's hard-won local identity.

Unlike Mrs Thatcher, Dennis believed in and treasured 'community'. Bilston, to him, was far more than the set of buildings, streets and alleyways described above. It was a vibrant pulsating community, whose love of life was displayed on a daily basis in the comfort and affection of its homesteads, the neighbourly greeting and gossip on its street, the bonhomie of its clubs, pubs, and day centres, the banter of its market traders, and the wry humour and solidarity of its workplaces. Dennis venerated the vigour and vitality of his Bilston community and drew his strength and sense of purpose from its long-established roots.

Social improvement, he thought, required a personal and practical investment in community, involving co-operation with neighbours on projects to better the human condition.[10] Just in case there was any danger of inadvertently forgetting the importance of the industrial past in this affirmation, on the 12th April 2009, the Bilston Community Association (of which Dennis had been president since his election as MP in 1987) erected a plaque at the end of the High Street to commemorate the 30th anniversary of the closure of the steel works, which had cast its last steel billet on 12 April 1979.

In hindsight, we could not help comparing Dennis's success in driving the sponsorship of a modern sculpture park in Bilston, based on his communitarian socialist vision, with Charles Saatchi's private patronage of his own London Gallery of Contemporary Art. We experienced no difficulty in evaluating the relative social impact and worth that each had achieved.

More recently in 2012, Dennis spearheaded the successful campaign to oppose the Boundary Commission's proposals to dismember the Bilston area, which previously sat in the Wolverhampton South East parliamentary constituency. The commission's sixth review would have seen the precious heartland of Bilston carved up and distributed between four new neighbouring electoral areas, thus destroying its political integrity. Determined Bilstonians took a coach to Birmingham to plead their case at a hearing of the commission. Their lobbying succeeded in getting the proposals changed.

**Wolverhampton achieves city status**

It would be wrong to give the impression that Dennis's efforts on behalf of Bilston led him to neglect the interests of Wolverhampton as a whole. His concern was never 'heritage', or in pursuing a narrow parochialism. He wished only to secure a larger slice of the cake for those at the periphery.[11] Bilston might indeed lie on the outskirts of Wolverhampton but, as his struggle to save the steel works and his time in parliament had shown him, Wolverhampton and the Black Country were themselves on the periphery of power, and their gravitational pull on economic and human capital was in serious decline.

Dennis placed himself at the forefront of the struggle to attract inward investment and money for social projects to the borough and the region, seeing the need to rebrand or repackage the area to assist in the process. From the time he entered parliament, as evidenced by his maiden speech, he did his best to draw attention to the positive features of the constituency he represented. Roger Lawrence, Wolverhampton council leader, drew attention to how Dennis had fought the borough's corner with Tory ministers time and time again, and then worked closely with the Labour Group to strengthen its case with the new Labour government.[12]

To Dennis's mind, one way of lending a hand was to win Wolverhampton the status of a city. As early as 1966, when Bilston and Wolverhampton were amalgamated, the *Wolverhampton Chronicle* had carried an article headlined

'The town that is a city in all but name'.[13] The idea of this historical West Midlands town, with its population of one-quarter of a million, becoming a city appealed to Dennis, not simply for the status it would confer but, as he later explained, to "bring the community together and...be a boost for Wolverhampton's economy".[14]

Wolverhampton's application for city status, which had failed in 1992, was duly dusted down and improved upon, and submitted in 1999, along with 39 other applications, 27 from English towns, as part of the so-called 'Millennium Competition'. Accepting the importance of the submission for Wolverhampton's future prosperity, the town's three Labour MPs – Dennis, Ken Purchase and Jenny Jones – did their best to support it, making repeated representation to the ministers responsible, before the final selection of towns wended its way to the Palace.

On the 18th December 2000, the *Express & Star*, under the headline 'We're a city', announced Wolverhampton had become one of three 'millennium cities', along with Brighton and Hove, and Inverness, effective from the 31st January 2001.[15]

Dennis was quoted as saying that the honour would "achieve exactly the right psychological atmosphere...the feel-good factor...that something good has happened to the town".[16] Ken Purchase agreed that it would be "a real tonic for the town",[17] while the mayor hoped it would "attract a lot of inward investment into Wolverhampton. People would rather invest in a city than a town".[18]

Wolverhampton's success in the competition came as a surprise to many people. Unaware of the politics of the process, or Dennis's formidable persuasive powers, the bookies had seriously miscalculated Wolverhampton's chances.

# Chapter 14

## Beer lovers' champion

### The campaign for a full pint

Dennis always objected strongly to the longstanding scandal of beer and cider drinkers being served short measure in pubs.[1] Fifteen million beer and cider drinkers are still denied the protection of weights and measures legislation, which governs almost every other item in the sale of food and drink. Currently, customers buy a pint measure of beer and froth. The Campaign for Real Ale (CAMRA) claims that 9 out of every 10 pints sold in British pubs are less than 100 per cent liquid and that 1 in 4 pints is less than the brewing industry's own guidelines of 95% minimum liquid. Licensees are apparently selling an extra 200 million pints of beer each year than they buy in, with a wholesale value of £130 million.

On 18 June 1997, Dennis, supported by eleven other members, including local MPs, Jenny Jones and Ken Purchase, introduced the Weights and Measures (Beer and Cider) Private Members' bill, to amend the law of weights and measures in relation to measures of beer and cider.

It was not for the first time that Dennis had intervened in the legislative process concerning the consumption of beer in public houses. During the discussion of the 1988 Licensing bill, he, together with Ann Taylor and the late Robin Corbett, moved a successful amendment to increase drinking-up time from 10 to 20 minutes which, although only a modest proposal, made the business of drinking up at the end of the evening a little more dignified.

Dennis's bill on fair measures was read for the first time and ordered to be read a second time on 12 December 1997.[2] Eric Forth, the Conservative MP for Bromley and Chiselhurst, aired his objection to the bill at the standing committee on 11 March 1998, claiming that there was infinite variety in the head of beers and their liquid content.

## Eric Forth objects

Dennis countered by drawing attention to the highly unsatisfactory situation regarding the sale of draught beers and cider, with the courts ruling that the gas contained in the head could be included when measuring how much beer the consumer had received, making it very difficult to bring successful prosecutions for short measure. When read again at the report stage on 3 July 1998, Eric Forth shouted 'object', causing the bill to fall.[3]

Forth was not only opposed to the workers receiving a full measure of liquid beer, but was fond of filibustering Labour motions, causing Labour members to sit late into the night. He was against the Sex Equality bill, wanted to bring back capital punishment, opposed the BBC spending money on the 1988 Nelson Mandela concert, and government funding of research into the treatment of aids, saying that it was largely self inflicted - altogether an objectionable character. It should come as no surprise that Dennis, in turn, objected strongly to him.

## CAMRA award

Dennis received the campaign for Real Ale's National Award for his efforts in addressing the evil of the short pint. CAMRA members were urged to write directly to Eric Forth to tell him what they thought of his objection. To its great credit, the Wolverhampton and Dudley Brewery (Banks's), on Dennis's home ground of Wolverhampton, supported his campaign for a full pint, and introduced an oversize glass to accommodate the beer head, together with a marker line to indicate the liquid measure.[4] Eventually, however, it abandoned the use of lined glasses in its 200 managed pubs on the grounds that they were incompatible with other suppliers' branded glasses and the new beer-dispensing systems.

**Dennis ale**

To commemorate his campaign, CAMRA and Banks's collaborated to produce bottles of '100% DENNIS ale', with labels explaining 'Dennis Turner MP is the beer lovers' champion and the beer is brewed in recognition of his tireless campaign to secure an honest pint law – Alcoholic 9.1% vol.'[5]

Dennis recognised, of course, the importance of drinking real ale in an ale house or pub – a place which existed for that specific purpose. The beer tasted even better if the ale happened to be brewed on the same premises! The CAMRA agenda entailed not only campaigning for a full pint of real ale, but acting to save the traditional British public house as the ideal environment in which to drink it. It was for this reason that Dennis was an enthusiastic supporter and vice-chair of the All-Party Parliamentary Save the Pub Group, dedicated to preserving and protecting the British pub.[6]

This chapter has deliberately been served as short measure. Dennis made it very clear to us that he did not wish to be remembered only, or mainly, as 'the beer lover's champion', and rejected emphatically the suggestion that this epithet should serve as a possible title for this biography - or indeed our proposal that it be called 'Fair Measures'. He saw his life as having a far more serious moral and political purpose than that.

He was much prouder of his contribution to the provision of the Haven, a refuge for women, who are so often the victims of a male violence fuelled by excessive beer and alcohol consumption. Nevertheless, gambling and beer drinking were working people's pleasures, which could be safely enjoyed by most in moderation. He would be the first to defend them, but it was ever incumbent on individuals to exercise restraint in the cause of the common good.[7]

# Chapter 15

## The bold Baron Bilston

### Standing down from the Commons

Just before the general election in 2006, when he was aged 62, Dennis announced he was standing down from the Commons. He had not been in the best of health for some time, and was awaiting an operation on his diaphragm to help improve his breathing.[1]

While he enjoyed his parliamentary work, which he attended to assiduously, he would have been 67 by the time of the next general election, and felt it was time to make way for a younger and healthier candidate.

### Baron Bilston

Recognising his worth to the Labour Party at Westminster, Tony Blair chose to recommend him for a life peerage, an honour that Dennis accepted only after careful consideration of the possibilities for continuing to contribute to the work of parliament. Dennis was made a peer on the 20th June 2005 and entered the Lords on the 5th July 2005.

In accordance with time-honoured custom, Dennis visited the Garter King of Arms to acquire his baronial title, making clear, so he thought, that he wished to be called 'Baron Turner of Bilston'. Unfamiliar, as are most, with mediaeval protocol, Dennis may not have expressed his lordly intentions with sufficient vigour. He discovered, too late, that he had been saddled with the repetitive territorial title of 'Baron Bilston of Bilston in the County of West Midlands'.

Asked why he had chosen that title in preference to taking the name of his birth place, 'Bradley', he pointed out that no one outside of the Black Country would know that it was pronounced 'Braidley'. He reckoned that it was certainly better to be known as 'Bilston' than 'Bradley' (as in 'Bradley Wiggins').[2]

Even so, his new title created a great deal of confusion among his acquaintances, correspondents and former constituents. He and his wife, Pat, were greeted with a bewildering variety of titles, including 'Lord Den', 'Lord Turner', 'Lord Bilston, Old Cock', 'Lord Bilston of Bradley', 'Mar Mite, his Lordship', etc., and 'Lady Pat', 'Lady Pattie', 'Lady Turner', 'Mi Lady', 'Mi Lady, Love,' etc. All were gracefully acknowledged without ever any attempt at correction. Dennis and Pat confessed to being disconcerted, however, by clumsy efforts to bow or curtsey, whether they were made in jest or, far worse, as genuine gestures of supplication.

### Hired ermine

Dennis had no interest whatsoever in the pomp and flummery of the Lords. He hired his ermine for the investiture, but never purchased a robe, or coat of arms, regarding them as an expensive extravagance.[3] He saw his position as merely an opportunity to continue serving the cause of Labour, the country, and the people of Wolverhampton.

As a matter of fact, he found the title 'Lord Bilston' somewhat of an embarrassment, persistently requesting his friends to go on calling him 'Dennis'. When in hospital in 2013, he rejected the medical staff's persistent attempts to address him as 'my Lord' or 'Lord Bilston', insisting that they refer to him only as 'Dennis' or 'Mr Turner', and explaining to them that titles of rank were wholly inappropriate among NHS patients.[4]

Nevertheless, Dennis and Pat were delighted with the competition organised by local primary schools to design them a coat of arms, one boy drawing a shield with a bottle of Banks's beer. They visited Graiseley School to present the award to the winner.[5]

## The Barnsby attack

Despite his refusal to stand on ceremony, he was condemned by some on the far-left for accepting a peerage which they saw as symbolic of privilege, and the antithesis of the social equality he professed to be fighting for. When it was announced that Dennis was in line to be made a Freeman of the City of Wolverhampton, George Barnsby, a notorious local historian, communist, and left-wing political activist, wrote a letter to the council (which was posted on line) roundly condemning the privileges and perks of a peerage, "which no self-respecting left-wing MP" would ever have accepted.[6]

Barnsby was, as usual, very wide of the mark. Many of Dennis's constituents, particularly those who knew him personally, considered the honour to be a well-deserved recognition of his life-time of service to the people of Wolverhampton. Most informed Labour Party members recognised that, under the current constitution, legislation had to be approved by both Houses of Parliament, and Dennis was continuing to serve his party as a working peer.

In this respect, Dennis's attendance was as regular and his voting record as consistent as it had been in the Commons. He travelled down to London on every occasion that parliament was in session.

## House of Lords reform

On taking his seat, Dennis found himself at the heart of the debate on Lords reform and, together with his friend, Bruce Grocott, Labour Chief Whip in the Lords, played an active role in the Campaign for an Effective Second Chamber.[7] The campaign aims to make the Lords more effective, to participate in the debate on its reform and to assess the options for change. Dennis recognised the essential role that the second chamber plays in scrutinising legislation. Election for seats, he believed, would deplete the Chamber of the expertise and experience it had accumulated over time, and directly undermine the democratic legitimacy and primacy of the Commons.

Alternatively, the Lords could more easily be reformed by making the remaining hereditary peers into life peers, by introducing an appointment commission which selected peers on the basis of merit, and by expelling abusers, mis-users and those guilty of serious criminal offences.

## Opposition to the alternative vote

Dennis was also a vigorous opponent of the Liberal Democrat proposal to alter the first-past-the-post electoral system in favour of the alternative vote, and helped mobilise the Upper House against AV.[8]

The alternative vote is a preferential system where electors rank the candidates in order of preference by putting a 1 by their first choice, a 2 by the second, etc. Candidates are elected outright if they gain more than 50 per cent of first preference votes but, if not, the candidate with the least first preferences is eliminated, and his or her votes are redistributed according to the second preference, a process continued, until someone achieves the 50 per cent necessary to be elected.

Dennis saw very little wrong with the first-past-the-post system and believed AV would throw up a candidate that no one really wanted, favouring minority parities, such as the Liberal Democrats, UKIP and the BNP (even though the BNP supported the no vote).[9] When, as part of the Conservative/Liberal Democrat coalition agreement, the alternative vote proposal was put to a referendum on 5 May 2011, it was rejected by more than two thirds of the electorate.

## Dennis's role in amending the Pedlars Act 1871

One of Dennis's achievements was to steer four local and personal bills through the House of Lords in one day – the 3rd December 2012.[10] These bills, submitted by Canterbury City Council, Leeds City Council, Nottingham City Council and Reading Borough Council, aimed to make changes to the Pedlars Act 1871, but had been extensively modified in committee. (Pedlars differ from street traders in that they are itinerant, moving from place to place and trading while travelling. They are not allowed to set up stalls and wait for people to approach.)

Dennis, with his background as vice president of the Local Government Association, and chair of its Markets Committee, was familiar with the issues involved and had piloted the bills through committee, making sure that the rights of pedlars were not unduly restricted, that there were measures to prevent obstruction to the highway, with restrictions to the size of pedlars' stalls, and that while fixed-penalty fines might be levied, councils would not be allowed to seize pedlars' goods. The four bills were also standardised to prevent piecemeal modification of national law by private legislation.

After Dennis had drawn the Lords' attention to the main points of the four bills, they were passed and returned to the Commons.[11]   Dennis believed that the representation before the Lords of four private bills in one day was unprecedented.[12]

# Chapter 16

## Till we have built Jerusalem

### Celebrating the socialist legacy

Despite his disdain for the pomp and ceremony of the House of Lords, Dennis remained acutely conscious all his life of the importance of the performing arts to political life, and was well known for his set party pieces, not only at the aforementioned 'works outings', when he and David Clelland entertained Labour MPs, but on other important occasions, such as at the celebration of a Labour Party victory, after the count, or at the club afterwards, or when he was called upon to give an impromptu speech at a dinner, wedding reception, launch, or award-giving ceremony. Roger Lawrence, the Wolverhampton council leader, looked back on how "Dennis's oratory lifted the party in difficult times and his singing was the high point of many a post-election event at the Springvale club."[1]

When there was a Labour victory to celebrate, Dennis would lead the faithful with a loud but melodious rendering of the Red Flag, often following up with an encore, consisting of a verse or two of Jerusalem, the anthem of the Suffragists, which for him was a favourite.[2] (He particularly liked and emphasised the line about 'building Jerusalem' although the part of England in which he had been brought up was neither green nor particularly pleasant.)

### *The Red Flag*

'The people's flag is deepest red,
It shrouded oft our martyr'd dead,
And ere their limbs grew stiff and cold,
Their hearts' blood dyed its ev'ry fold.

It well recalls the triumphs past,
It gives the hope of peace at last,

The banner bright, the symbol plain
Of human right and human gain.

With head uncovered, swear we all
To bear it onward till we fall,
Come dungeons dark or gallows grim,
This song shall be our parting hymn.

Then raise the scarlet standard high,
Within its shade we'll live or die,
Though cowards flinch and traitors sneer,
We'll keep the red flag flying here.'

### Jerusalem

'I will not cease from Mental Fight,
Nor shall my Sword Sleep in my hand,
Till we have built Jerusalem
In England's green and pleasant land.'

Apart from the obvious, Dennis had his own particular repertoire of inspirational hymns and verses, often reflecting his religious inclination, but usually having a political or communitarian theme. One of these, which he sang to us in hospital, but which had been used, we are sure, at school assemblies, was Daniel O'Donnell's At the end of the day, with Dennis particularly relishing the line about 'the new dawn' beginning to break.[3]

### At the end of the day

'At the end of the day just kneel and say
'Thank you, Lord, for my work and play.'
I've tried to be good for I know that I should,
That's my prayer for the end of the day.

So when the new dawn begins to break
Just lift up your eyes, let your heart awake,
Be ready to meet what the day may send
And be ready to greet every man as a friend.

Nobody knows what a power you have found,
So do what you can for the others around,
Carry them high when they seem to be low,
As on your way you go.'

## The Rubaiyat

Dennis was particularly fond of quoting from Edward Fitzgerald's *The Rubaiyat of Omar Khayyam*, selecting especially the following verse to inspire new and radical socialist initiatives:

'Ah Love! Could thou and I with fate conspire
To grasp this sorry Scheme of Things entire,
Would not we shatter it to bits – and then
Remould it nearer to the Heart's Desire!'[4]

He did, indeed, quote the whole verse in his maiden speech to the Commons on the 2nd July 1987.[5]

## The Socialist ABC

While Dennis was familiar with the Socialist ABC, he was inclined to leave this more doctrinaire element of the 'works outing' repertoire to David Clelland, a 'bonny bonny bairn' from the part of the country referred to.[6]

'When that I was and a little, tiny boy,
Me daddy said to me,
'The time has come, me bonny bonny bairn,
To learn your ABC."

Now Daddy was lodge chairman
In the coalfields of the Tyne
And his ABC was different
From the Enid Blyton kind.

He sang, "A is for Alienation
That made me the man that I am, and

B's for the Boss who's a Bastard,
A Bourgeois who don't give a damn.

C is for Capitalism,
The bosses' reactionary creed, and

D's for Dictatorship, laddie,
But the best proletarian breed.

E is for Exploitation
That workers have suffered so long, and

F is for old Ludwig Feuerbach,
The first one to say it was wrong.'

& etc.

### It couldn't be done

On less triumphant occasions, when things hadn't gone to plan, Dennis resorted to his own parody of Edgar Albert Guest's 'It couldn't be done':

'They said it could not be done,
That many men had tried.
Some stood with heads hung low,
While others sat and cried.

They said it could not be done
And everybody knew it.
But he was his father's son.
He could not turn and run.

He had to tackle that which could not be done,
But he bloody well couldn't do it.'[7]

This always brought a laugh even to those of us who had heard it many times
before.

# Chapter 17

## Out of darkness cometh light

Wolverhampton's motto, 'Out of darkness cometh light' serves as a suitable metaphor for the life of Dennis Turner, who emerged from the industrial smog of Bradley and the Black Country to shine as a beacon of progressive activity brightening the life of the people living and working there. Knowing what it was like to be poor, Dennis grew up with an unshakeable mission to abolish poverty, not just his own, of course, but that of everyone in his community. The back-to-back house in which he was born was overcrowded and damp, with a tap in the yard. From a very young age, he saw the collective provision of council housing as the only practical solution to his community's need for secure shelter.

An intelligent boy who failed the eleven-plus and left school at fifteen to pay for his keep at home, Dennis was a relentless advocate of comprehensive education for all, with opportunities for life-long study – especially for people of working age. For him, education and training were, first and foremost, a means of developing people's natural capacity and understanding, and making them more rational and considerate human beings, capable of contributing in full measure to the grand scheme of things.

Dennis's knowledge of his father's job in the steel works, his own work in the rolling mill, and as a Betterware salesman, market trader, and stock taker, gave him a profound insight from a young age into the local workers' daily struggle to earn enough money to provide for themselves and their families. He understood that work was essential to economic self-sufficiency, and believed that a primary role of government was to manage an economy and industrial base in a way that guaranteed full employment opportunities and a living wage for everyone – especially the young, the old, and the vulnerable.

This would entail a socialist economic arrangement, best summed up for Dennis by Sidney Webb's 1917 declaration of purpose, better known now as

Clause IV: 'to secure for the workers, by hand or by brain, the full fruits of their industry and the most equitable distribution thereof that may be possible upon the basis of the common ownership of the means of production, distribution and exchange, and the best obtainable system of popular administration and control of each industry or service'.

Dennis realised from the variety of his own jobs and work experiences, that each industry might indeed require its own unique form of popular administration, leading him to adopt his own fourfold approach, as previously outlined. In essence, the socialist economy he envisaged involved not only the nationalisation of the mega-industries, such as the railways, coal, and steel, but the development of municipal enterprises and co-operatives to provide the essentials of daily life. There would be plenty of space left for a private sector to act entrepreneurially, to innovate, and to provide other goods.

It was important, too, to expand and furnish facilities for individuals and families who had special burdens to cope with, such as disability, sickness, mental illness, domestic violence, crime, discrimination of various kinds, and homelessness.

Stemming directly from raw experience, this framework of belief, formulated in the context of a social interpretation of Christian teaching and within a left-leaning family and local community, formed the springboard for all Dennis's subsequent political activity at local and national level. Nevertheless, his vision of socialism retained a distinctly-romantic William Morris arts-and-crafts aura. But for his steely resolve, stiffened by industrial action, Dennis could easily have been mistaken for an Arcadian character strayed from a film version of *News from Nowhere*.

Dennis was always a persuader, doer, and leader, who rapidly learned the knack of taking people with him just as far as he knew he could take them. He was always persistent, never resting until the task he had in mind was completed. His confidence, skills in leadership, organisation and management were improved by every successive campaign, first in the struggle to keep open the Bilston steel works, later during the great steel strike of 1980, and then in setting up the Springvale Co-operative. By this time, of course, he had been elected to Wolverhampton Council and the West Midlands County Council and used these positions to maximum effect.

His seven-year stint as chair of Wolverhampton Social Services Committee is remarkable for the number of new and creative initiatives he launched to support vulnerable groups, such as old people in need of care, children and adults with special learning difficulties, victims of domestic violence, homeless Asian women and young black men, and single homeless adults. In 1987, Dennis entered parliament as a Labour MP, determined to benefit the people of Wolverhampton by ensuring the town received its fair share of government funding and favours. For a full 27 years, from his arrival at Westminster, the welfare of Wolverhampton residents remained his paramount purpose.

His sincere and unswerving commitment to his Black Country constituents and their origins, culture, values, causes, pastimes, and pleasures, resulted in his parliamentary colleagues regarding him as the quintessential embodiment of working-class authenticity, trade union solidarity, co-operative endeavour, municipal welfare, and practical socialism. Like the other Dennis, his friend, Dennis Skinner, he soon became a living icon of Labour integrity, helpfully augmented in his case by his genuine passion for real ale, greyhounds, and horse racing.

Andrew Rawnsley, political journalist and broadcaster, columnist for *The Observer*, and author of books on the phenomenon of New Labour, summed it up neatly. There were three kinds of Labour: 'Old Labour, New Labour, and the Real Labour of Dennis Turner'. [1]

Why so real? For those on the Left, Dennis's authenticity related to his old-fashioned socialism. After all was said and done, he held on steadfastly to a belief in the merits of the common ownership of the means of production, and remained wholeheartedly committed to slaying William Beveridge's five giants of squalor, ignorance, want, idleness, and disease, by means of a collectivist welfare state, available on equal terms to everyone. He never wavered in seeing himself as a member of the industrial working class, whose interests he constantly strove to represent, whether in the capacity of an active trade unionist, co-operator, councillor, or member of parliament. In that last role, he was one of a tiny minority – less than 5 per cent of current MPs has ever engaged in manual work. And he regarded it as a privilege to represent and campaign on behalf of the constituency, and the working-class community in which he was born, brought up, worked, lived all his life, and had chosen to die. This is why Dennis personified 'Real Labour'.

From the Opposition backbenches, Dennis contributed, as far as he could, to formulating policy on unemployment, education (especially further education), and local government. In 1997, when Labour took power, Dennis became parliamentary private secretary to Clare Short, the Secretary of State for International Development. He assisted her in setting up the new DfID and adopting the 'millennium development goals', aimed at using government overseas aid money, not for short-term commercial purposes, but to eradicate directly poverty, hunger, disease, and ignorance. Dennis could now pursue these goals, so dear to his heart, not only in the Black Country and at national level, but on the global stage. As a fervent socialist internationalist, he described his work at the DfID as a truly wonderful period in his life. His mentor, after all, had been the illustrious Bob Edwards, who had fought as a captain with the International Brigade in Spain.

Dennis had a profound and lifelong commitment to the cause of international development. After Fairtrade tea and coffee were introduced at the DfID and in the House of Commons, Dennis persuaded Wolverhampton to become a Fairtrade City, and continued to chair the Wolverhampton Fairtrade Partnership until his death on the 25th February 2014.

In his politics, Dennis was consistent and persistent to the very end. Any inconsistency in his voting record as an MP can be explained by his firm belief in the primacy of his chosen political vehicle – the Labour Party –

without which he knew that by himself he could achieve little or nothing.

For his lifetime of service to the country and community, Dennis received many accolades, so numerous, in fact, that only a few can be recorded here. His elevation to the peerage might indeed be regarded as a high honour but, as has been noted, Dennis was inclined to regard his position in the Lords as just a job, albeit an important one. He felt very privileged, however, when a competition was held in Wolverhampton primary schools to design him a baronial coat of arms – one entry featuring a bottle of his favourite Banks's Mild – acclaim which he rated far above anything the Garter King of Arms could ever have bestowed on him.

There was, of course, the tribute of the 100% Dennis ale brewed by the Wolverhampton and Dudley Breweries and presented to him by the Campaign for Real Ale in recognition of his campaign for an honest pint. This gesture, we know, he greatly appreciated, although he never wanted to be thought of as merely as a beer-drinkers' champion.

He was proud, too, of the wall plaque signed and presented by Ed Miliband, Labour Leader, for organising the parliamentary 'works outing' over many years.

What Dennis valued most, however, was the love and appreciation of his local community and the recognition that he was afforded by the adults, the children and the dogs everywhere he went in Bradley, Bilston, Wolverhampton, the Black Country, and the West Midlands.

The conferment of the freedom of the City of Wolverhampton on the 20th December 2006 meant a great deal to him. He felt a little awed at finding himself on a list that, in more recent times, included Sir Charles Mander (1945), Sir Charles Wheeler (1958), Denise Lewis OBE (2000), and Sir Jack Hayward (2003).

In 2006, the University of Wolverhampton made Dennis (along with the poet, Benjamin Zephania), a Doctor of Letters, which he considered a great honour, especially in the light of his eleven-plus failure more than half a century earlier. Unlike some others, he made no attempt to add 'doctor' to his cv or title. He shared the authors' scepticism about the merits of honorary degrees, revealed when he joked afterwards that all he now needed were honorary GCSEs and A levels.[2]

**Famous son**

More recently, in September 2013, Wolverhampton Partners in Progress accorded their Wolverhampton Famous Sons and Daughters Awards to seven of the City's most renowned citizens at a presentation ceremony at the Molineux Stadium. The seven selected for this honour were:

Steve Bull, footballer, Wolverhampton,

Dave Hill, lead guitarist, the Slade,

Denise Lewis, Olympic heptathlete and gold medallist,

Liam Payne, singer, One Direction,

Kristian Thomas, Olympic gymnast,

Dennis Turner, former Wolverhampton MP and member of the House of Lords, and

Bert Williams, former England goalkeeper.

Dennis gave the acceptance speech on behalf of all the recipients. Significantly, he was the only politician on the list of Wolverhampton's famous, which consisted otherwise of celebrity sports personalities and pop stars.[3]

**Tributes from councillors**

Councillor Roger Lawrence, leader of Wolverhampton City Council, was in no doubt that his contribution to the politics of the city had been immense: "And I do mean the city, for though a son of Bilston, Dennis would come out wherever help was needed and, when in my ward, reminded me he had worked in Whitmore Reans many years before as a door-to-door salesman.

He was still remembered on the doorsteps and could have sold a bagful of brushes while out canvassing. In an era when both parties tend to stack their benches with graduates who have been special advisers, he might have seemed to belong to an earlier age. But his wise advice, friendship and loyalty stood the test of time. Like Bilston steel, they don't make them like that any more."[4]

Councillor Ian Claymore, a former mayor of Wolverhampton, told us that "Dennis, both as a councillor and an MP, has, more than any other person I know, left a lasting legacy to the residents of the city, in the form of its economic developments, public buildings, housing, social services, sporting, leisure and cultural facilities".[5]

Professor Mel Chevannes, a former councillor colleague, who became a close friend, described how she had first met Dennis: "In September 1981, when I was elected to Wolverhampton Council, Dennis was deputy leader. I was struck immediately by his friendly, relaxed and sociable personality. He went out of his way to encourage me and help me find my feet on the council. When council leader, John Bird, appointed me chair of the Social Services Committee, I asked Dennis to come back onto the committee, which he had chaired for so long, to give me the benefit of his experience and local knowledge. He agreed immediately to join, offering me, on every occasion, his full and unqualified support, especially when I was trying to implement a full reorganisation of the Social Services Department. From then on, he became a dear friend, whose advice and support I knew I could always count upon. I miss him immensely."[6]

The mayor of Wolverhampton, Councillor Mulkinderpal Jaspal, said that Dennis had been an outstanding councillor, MP, and member of the Lords: "He was one of the rare individuals who was born and grew up in the area he was to represent... Everyone knew him and he knew everyone."[7]

The day after Dennis died, the flags at Wolverhampton Civic Centre (the union jack, the city flag, and the flag of the co-op) were flown at half mast as a tribute to the man who had served on the authority from 1966 to 1986 and who had led the successful campaign for city status. Meanwhile in Bilston, a minute's silence, followed by applause, was held at the Bilston Town versus Dudley Town football match. But Dudley still won, 4 goals to 1.

## Tributes from parliamentarians

On learning that Dennis was seriously ill, former prime minister, Tony Blair, sent us the following message: "I always regard Dennis as one of the unspoken heroes of the parliamentary Labour Party. He has always been loyal, unassuming, utterly committed to, and in touch with the people of Wolverhampton. He was always supportive to me, especially during the tougher periods of government. I was delighted to be able to recommend him as a Labour working peer."8

Likewise, Neil Kinnock, Labour leader from 1983 to 1992, and longstanding friend, emailed to say that:

"Dennis epitomises all that is best about the Labour movement. He is a true democratic socialist with a special mixture of common sense and enlightenment, with his feet on the ground and his eyes on the horizon of possibility. All this comes naturally to him. It hasn't come from scholarly research, worthy though that is. It comes from the life he leads and his convictions of justice which are solidly rooted in experience.

He knows that, whenever that combination is lost, we cut ourselves adrift from the people and causes we exist to serve. He understands that truth in his mind, heart and gut, which makes him both a wise man and an activist – in the best sense of that over-used but under-comprehended word.

Best of all, he has proved this with a lifetime of service to the people he has represented at every level. And he always does it with a sensitivity and modesty, without any of the pomp and self-importance, which too often affects those who want public attention for doing what is no more than their plain duty. These qualities made him a wonderful MP, because they mean that he combines hard-headed loyalty with trenchant private criticism which, when delivered in that metal-bashing Black Country accent, hammer home the point that he wants to make to a 'bruther' towards whom he didn't feel very brotherly."[9]

Knowing that Dennis was ill, Ed Miliband, Labour leader and leader of the Opposition, wrote to convey his good wishes: "I know what a strong spirit you have ... with all my positive thoughts, Ed."[10]

Lord Bruce Grocott, Dennis's close colleague and fellow peer, spoke of Dennis's long journey, from the poverty of his childhood upbringing, to the Wolverhampton Council, and then to the House of Commons and the House of Lords: "Throughout it all, Dennis went unchanged, true to everything he had always stood for, while achieving so much for others. If only there were more Dennis Turners in parliament. What good news that would be, both for the Labour Party and for the country!" [11]

David Clelland, now retired from parliament, considered Dennis to be a remarkable and unique man: "I have been proud to have been his close friend over the past 27 years. I have learned a lot about the Co-op movement and the Black Country and its history from Dennis, who is always so proud of his background and the people he grew up with and lived amongst. He is immensely popular and well-liked inside and outside of parliament, not only by MPs and Peers of all political persuasions, but by the hundreds of staff and workers in the Palace of Westminster, who Dennis always has time for and is on first-name terms with."[12]

Dennis Skinner, MP for Bolsover since 1970, former coal miner and son of a miner sacked after the General Strike of 1926, wrote to Dennis during his illness, urging him to keep up the good fight: "You are always in our thoughts because you are a true product of the working class - always proud of your roots!"[13]

Former MP for Wolverhampton North East, Ken Purchase, a friend for over 45 years, spoke of Dennis's "unsurpassed personal charm and decency" and "his lovely way with people, always taking them with him".[14]

After visiting Dennis a number of times in hospital, Pat McFadden, who succeeded him as MP for Wolverhampton South East, told us: "Every time I have seen him, he has talked of the next step in treatment and what's going to happen after that. I haven't ever heard him say anything negative at any point. He is relentlessly positive about life, as shown in the way he has coped with his illness in recent weeks. He is hugely grateful to the NHS staff who have looked after him. One of his favourite sayings is to 'go through life making friends, not enemies', and that's an important insight into his character. If you ever find yourself in disagreement with him there is never any bitterness or hostility. He enjoys life, likes the company of people, and wants to see the best in everyone. In conversation, he looks for the point of agreement, not the point of disagreement, and that's a great trait."[15]

**Dennis's funeral**

On Wednesday the 12th March 2014, the hearse bearing Dennis's coffin, heaped with wreaths of red and white carnations, left Aubyn in King Street, Bradley, on its short journey to St Leonard's Church in the centre of Bilston. The procession of the Bilston Co-operative Service's five shiny-black limousines moved slowly along Lichfield Street, where the ordinary people of the town had gathered on the pavements to show their respect. The cars turned into Church Street and came to a halt outside the church. The bearers, led by Brendon and Steve Mullings, carried the coffin into the crowded building, whose aisles and balconies were crammed to capacity.

Family members filed in to the seats reserved for them on the right hand side of the aisle in front of the rows of Wolverhampton councillors in gowns. Seated on the left was the Orpheus Male Voice Choir, next to a party of thirty or so of Dennis's friends and colleagues from the Palace of Westminster. Pat, Brendon and Jenny had compiled an attractive 16-page commemorative brochure for the occasion setting out the order of service, and including family photographs, favourite sayings, and the words of 'the Red Flag'.

As the coffin was brought forward, a recording of 'Amazing grace', sung by Jenny and her friend, Elaine, was played. After the minister's welcome, the congregation rose to sing, 'All things bright and beautiful,' the simple hymn that Dennis cherished.

The tributes came next. Son, Brendon, and brother, Bert Turner, spoke from their hearts of their love for Dennis, which brought tears to everyone's eyes. Professor Mel Chevannes recalled Dennis's hand in fashioning and improving Wolverhampton's local social, education and health services. Ken Purchase told of Dennis's political struggles, of his love for the words of William Morris, and how he and Dennis had so often tried to put the world to rights. Pat McFadden paid tribute to Dennis's unwavering loyalty to the Labour Party and how, as his parliamentary successor, he would always be grateful for Dennis's unstinting support and friendship. Lord Grocott praised Dennis's political consistency in focusing throughout his parliamentary life on the same social issues – poverty, unemployment, housing and education – with a view to alleviating the lot of the common people.

The tributes were followed by a lusty rendering of Dennis's favourite hymn, 'Jerusalem' – with plenty of emphasis given to what he had succeeded in building before he ceased 'from mental fight'.

Family and friends then left for the interment at Hall Green Cemetery in Bradley. The heavy cloud and mist of the morning cleared, and the sun shone brightly and beautifully, as Dennis's body was lowered into its final resting place, not more than a quarter of a mile from his childhood home in Powell Place, Bradley.

Drawing comfort from the knowledge that Dennis would have lent his wholehearted approval to this perfect send-off, the mourners adjourned for drinks, sandwiches and slices of pork pie to Dennis's other favourite haunt: the Springvale Sports and Social Club on Millfields Road, Bilston.

# Acknowledgments

In December 2013, after Dennis had undergone some serious surgery, my wife, Mel, and I proposed to him that it was high time he produced an account of his life, work and achievements, to serve as an inspiration to his family, and friends, and as a contribution to the history of the labour movement. In the course of the following two months, we visited him almost every day and took notes, as he enthusiastically recalled events of significance from his early childhood, through adulthood as a steel worker, councillor and MP, until his retirement from the Commons and acceptance of a seat in the Lords as a working peer.

Dennis only trusted us to write this book because he believed that we shared his socialist vision, and had participated for well over forty years in the self-same struggle to improve the lives of the people of Wolverhampton and the Black Country. Mel, in particular, found Dennis a most loyal and supportive colleague and friend when they served together as councillors. We are profoundly grateful to him for sharing his confidences with us, forcing us to keep pace with him, and making sure that the project was completed before time was called.

We hope our account proves us worthy of his trust and does justice to the story he wished to tell. With this goal in mind, we deliberately set out to produce more of a ghost-written autobiography, reflecting his priorities and perceptions, than a detached, considered, or critical biography, even though, given our own values and love for him, the eventual outcome would undoubtedly have been much the same. Dennis soon involved friends and family, urging them to co-operate fully with us in the project.

We are most grateful to Patricia Turner, Lady Bilston, for encouraging and facilitating our visits to home and hospitals, and providing us with the information, newspaper cuttings, and photographs we asked her for. Our thanks are due to Dennis and Pat's children, Brendon and Jenny, who told us about their Dad. Dennis's brother, Bert, helped fill in the background to events in Bradley, Bilston, Springvale, and the Bilston Steel Works. Bert's daughter, Lynne, impressed us with her practical kindness. We were assisted, too, by Dennis's nephew, Barry Nash, and his wife, Denise, who searched for photographs of Dennis in their family albums.

On hand, with anecdotes aplenty, were childhood friends, Len Bradbury and Frank Venton.

Recognising fully the therapeutic value and historical worth of the venture, Dennis's parliamentary colleagues were most willing to play their part. Tony Blair, David Clelland, Bruce Grocott, Neil Kinnock, Rob Marris, Pat McFadden, Ed Miliband, Dennis Skinner, and Ken Purchase knew and appreciated Dennis's inimitable contribution, and went out of their way to supply us with all that we asked for. Dennis was keen that we involve his parliamentary and constituency secretaries in this project. Hilary Davies and Jill Withers were delighted to be asked to participate and held him, as their employer, in high regard.

We also sought the views of Ian Claymore and Roger Lawrence, longstanding members of Wolverhampton Council, who worked alongside Dennis when he, too, was a councillor.

We thank Natalie Cole, the Exhibitions Officer at the Bilston Craft Gallery, and Kath Rees, Chief Executive of the Haven, Wolverhampton, for what they were able to tell us. We acknowledge the editor of the Wolverhampton *Express and Star* for generously allowing us to reproduce many of the pictures of Dennis appearing in this book.

There has been no insufficiency of informants or information. We could not include all that we were told, even by Dennis, nor indeed was all of it relevant. Nevertheless, almost every evening, we had more than enough to write up and word-process. Our main constraint has been one of time. We sought to complete the draft manuscript as fast as we could to enable Dennis to read, correct, amend and make further suggestions, chapter by chapter, discussing ever more changes at each visit to his bedside. Before he died, we had received his approval of drafts of all but the last chapter. More could have been written, of course, but it would have lacked the input, critical assessment, and political imprimatur of the man whom we were describing. Every evening, Mel, whom Dennis entirely trusted, made sure a new section was typed and run off for his approval.

Dennis, magnanimous as always, had his own idiosyncratic opinions about the content and substance of a biography, which we felt obliged to ignore as much as we could. Operating with the mindset of a co-operator, Dennis conceived of his life story as a list of good deeds done by those other people who had helped him in his various political struggles, enterprises and achievements. If we had not insisted, he would have featured as an understated and insignificant bystander in his own curriculum vitae. He was clearly incapable of blowing his own trumpet, or recognising, and even remembering, the significance of the contributions he had made, except, not surprisingly, in relation to Bilston.

We have conceded some ground to his curious views in Chapter 12, 'Friends in high places' and, in this section, 'Acknowledgments'. From these examples, the reader can well imagine how other chapters would have turned out, if we had done exactly as we were told.

Dennis wanted the final chapter of the book to consist entirely of a tribute to "our wonderful National Health Service", and to include a list of the names of doctors, nurses and other health professionals who treated him during his final illness. Suffice it here to thank Mr Balain, the surgeon, and the medical team at Oswestry, Mr Scofield and other medical staff at the Royal Shrewsbury, Dr Lal, Dennis's indispensible GP, and the pleasant Dr New, at the Bradley Health Centre, and the teams from Compton Hospice and Community Nursing, Wolverhampton.

Dennis insisted, however, that we acknowledge in full, Dr Grumett, Dr Fitzgerald, and all the staff of the Deanesly Centre, New Cross: Ward Manager

Sister Julie Banner, Sister Sylvia Lawrence, Charge Nurse Samson Gnayi, and nurses: Amy Brewerton, Jess Broomhall, Ena Dudek, Jesus Dulgar, Lorna Hinks, Linda Kenny, Heather Leonard, Sabrina Luther, Kayleigh Morgan, Lisa Ottley, Gaylord Rance, Theresa Sailsman, Liane Winsper, and health care assistants: Yvonne Campbell, Chris Davies, Teresa Davies, Tracey Fairfax-Henry, Debbie Mason, Marlene Nolan, Ms Shepherd, and ward clerk, Sue Kennedy, and ward assistant, Dawn Rose.

And let us thank, too, all the family members, friends, and well-wishers in Bradley, Bilston, the Black Country, Wolverhampton, the West Midlands, Westminster, and the World, for their messages of support. It was indeed remarkable to witness the sheer volume of the get-well cards and messages from people who had not only heard of Dennis, but knew him personally, had benefited from his friendship and help, and were genuinely concerned for his welfare.

As Ken Purchase, Dennis's longstanding political colleague, so succinctly summed it up: "I have never met anyone who didn't love Dennis".

Frank Reeves and Mel Chevannes
February 2014

# References

## Chapter 1     Chasing the rag-and-bone man

1. Turner, D., interview, 5 Dec 2013.
2. Ibid.
3. Ibid.
4. Turner, D., interview, 23 Jan 2014.
5. Turner, D., interview, 5 Dec 2013.
6. Ibid.
7. Ibid.
8. Turner, D., interview, 13 Dec 2013.
9. Ibid.
10. Turner, D., interview, 27 Dec 2013
11. Turner, D., interview, 5 Dec 2013.
12. Ibid.
13. Bradbury, L., interview, 13 Dec 2013.
14. Turner, D., interview, 3 Jan 2014.
15. Bradbury, L., interview, 13 Dec 2013.
16. Turner, D., interview, 3 Jan 2014.
17. Turner, D., interview, 5 Dec 2013.
18. Ibid.
19. Ibid.
20. Bradbury, L., interview, 13 Dec 2013.
21. Turner, D., interview, 26 Dec 2013.
22. Ibid.
23. Ibid.
24. Turner, D., interview, 13 Dec 2013.
25. Express & Star, deaths, 4 March 2014, p. 33.
26. Turner, D., interview, 26 Dec 2013.
27. Ibid.
28. Ibid.
29. Turner, D., interview, 9 Dec 2013.

30. Ibid.
31. Turner, D., interview, 3 Feb 2014.
32. Turner, D., interview, 9 Dec 2013.
33. Ibid.
34. Turner, D., interview, 23 Jan 2014.

**Chapter 2    Youth mayor of Bilston**

1. Turner, D., interview, 9 Dec 2013.
2. Ibid.
3. Turner, D., interview, 13 Dec 2013.
4. Ibid.
5. Barnsby, G.(1998), *Socialism in Birmingham and the Black Country 1850-1939*, Integrated Publishing Services, Wolverhampton, pp. 535-
6. Ibid.
7. Larkin, T. (undated), *Black Country Lives, Reflections of the Twentieth Century*, no page numbers.
8. Ibid.
9. Reeves, F. and Chevannes, M., various conversations with Frank Venton, 1995.
10. Turner, D., interview, 28 Dec 2013.
11. Turner, D., interview, 13 Dec 2013.
12. Ibid.
13. Ibid.
14. Turner, D., interview, 9 Dec 2013.
15. Ibid.

**Chapter 3    Wolverhampton's youngest councillor**

1. *Express & Star*, 29 March 1966.
2. *Express & Star*, 18 March 1966.
3. *Express & Star*, 22 March 1966.
4. Turner, D., interview, 9 Dec 2013.
5. Turner, D., interview, 27 Jan 2014.

6. Ibid.
7. Ibid.
8. Ibid.
9. Ibid.
10. Turner, D., interview, 9 Dec 2013.
11. Ibid.
12. Turner, D., interview, 30 Dec 2013.
13. Ibid.
14. Ibid.
15. Turner, D., interview, 30 Dec 2013.
16. Claymore, I., interview, 20 Jan 2014.
17. Turner, D., interview 30 Dec 2013.
18. Ibid.
19. Ibid.
20. Turner, D., interview, 27 Jan 2014.
21. Turner, D., interview, 30 Dec 2013.
22. Ibid.
23. Ibid.
24. Powell, E. (1969), *Freedom and Reality*, Kingswood, Surrey, Elliot Right Way, pp. 281-90.
25. Heilpern, J. (1968), 'Down among Mr Powell's constituents' in *The Observer*, 19 July 1968.
26. Reeves, F. (1989), *Race and Borough Politics*, Avebury, Gower, Aldershot.
27. Turner, D., interview, 17 Dec 2013.
28. Ibid.
29. Ibid.
30. Turner, D., interview, 2 Jan 2014.
31. Reeves, F., memory, 2 Jan 2014.

## Chapter 4   The council provides

1. Willis, P. et al.(1984) *The Youth Review. The Social Condition of Young People in Wolverhampton*, Wolverhampton Borough Council.

2.  Turner, D., interview, 1 Jan 2014.
3.  Turner, D., interview, 2 Jan 2014.
4.  Turner, D., interview, 1 Jan 2014.
5.  Wolverhampton Council, Social Services Committee Minutes, 21 July 1977.
6.  Wolverhampton Council, Social Services Committee Minutes, 8 Jan 1973.
7.  Wolverhampton Council, Social Services Committee Minutes, 18 March 1976.
8.  Turner, D., interview, 3 Feb 2014.
9.  Wolverhampton Council, Social Services Committee Minutes, 10 June 1976.
10. Wolverhampton Council, Social Services Committee Minutes, 24 July 1971.
11. Wolverhampton Council, Social Services Committee Minutes, 11 June 1973.
12. Wolverhampton Council, Social Services Committee Minutes, 10 June 1976.
13. Wolverhampton Council, Social Services Committee Minutes, 11 October 1974.
14. Wolverhampton Council, Social Services Committee Minutes, 10 June 1976.
15. Wolverhampton Council, Social Services Committee Minutes, 27 Jan 1978.
16. Rees, K., Chief Executive, The Haven, Wolverhampton, telephone call, 13 Jan 2014.
17. Ibid.
18. Turner, D., interview, 27 Dec 2013.
19. Turner, D., interview, 26 Dec 2013 & 28 Dec 2013.
20. Turner, D., interview, 26 Dec 2013.
21. Ibid.
22. Turner, D., interview, 27 Jan 2014.
23. Ibid.
24. Ibid.

25. Turner, D., interview, 17 Dec 2013.
26. Reeves, F., memory, 10 Dec 2013.

## Chapter 5    Seeing a man about a dog

1. Turner, T.H. (Bert), interview, 7 Jan 2014.
2. Turner, D., interview, 2 Jan 2014.
3. Ibid.
4. *The House*, Parliament's Weekly Magazine, All-Party Groups, a comprehensive guide, September 2011.
5. Turner, T.H. (Bert), interview, 7 Jan 2014.
6. Ibid.
7. Ibid.
8. Purchase, K., interview, 2 Jan 2014.
9. Turner, D., interview, 3 Jan 2014.
10. Turner, T.H. (Bert), interview, 7 Jan 2014.
11. Turner, P. (Pat), interview, 9 Dec 2013.
12. Ibid.
13. Ibid.
14. Ibid.
15. Ibid.
16. Purchase, K., interview, 2 Jan 2014.
17. Turner, D., interview, 3 Jan 2014.
18. Turner, T.H. (Bert), interview, 7 Jan 2014.
19. Clelland, D., interview, 3 Feb 2014.
20. Turner, T.H. (Bert), interview, 7 Jan 2014.
21. *Express & Star*, 26 Feb 2014, p. 18.
22. Turner, B. (Brendon), interview, 17 Jan 2014.
23. Mullings, J. (Jenny), interview, 28 Jan 2014.
24. Turner, D., interview, 3 Jan 2014.
25. Turner, B. (Brendon), interview, 17 Jan 2014.
26. Mullings, J. (Jenny), interview, 28 Jan 2014.
27. Ibid.
28. Ibid.

29. Ibid.
30. Turner, B. (Brendon), interview, 17 Jan 2014; Mullings, J. (Jenny), interview, 28 Jan 2014.
31. Mullings, J. (Jenny), interview, 28 Jan 2014.
32. Turner, B. (Brendon), interview, 17 Jan 2014.
33. Ibid.
34. Turner, T.H. (Bert), interview, 7 Jan 2014.

## Chapter 6 Saving the steel works

1. Turner, D., interview, 9 Dec 2013.
2. Ibid.
3. Turner, T.H. (Bert), interview, 7 Jan 2014.
4. Turner, D., interview, 9 Dec 2013.
5. Ibid.
6. Ibid.
7. Ibid.
8. Ibid.
9. Ibid.
10. Turner, D., interview, 3 Jan 2014.
11. Ibid.
12. Ibid.
13. Ibid.
14. Turner, D., interview, 9 Dec 2013.
15. Turner, D., interview, 2 Jan 2014.
16. Ibid.
17. Turner, T.H. (Bert), interview, 7 Jan 2014.
18. Turner, D., interview, 2 Jan 2014.
19. Turner, T.H. (Bert), interview, 7 Jan 2014.
20. Turner, D., interview, 2 Jan 2014.
21. *Lords Hansard*, *Lord Bilston* speaking on poverty, 8 May 2008, Column 733.
22. *The Times*, register, 5 Mar 2014, p. 52.

## Chapter 7    Dove on a dustcart

1.  Turner, D., interview, 17 Dec 2013.
2.  Ibid.
3.  Welfare Council Meeting at Social Centre, minutes, 8 Jan 1981, supplied by Turner, T.H. (Bert), 7 Jan 2014.
4.  Turner, D., interview, 17 Dec 2013.
5.  Ibid.
6.  Ibid.
7.  Ibid.
8.  Ibid.
9.  Ibid.
10. Ibid.
11. Turner, D., interview, 17 Dec 2013.
12. Purchase, K., interview, 2 Jan 2014.
13. Ibid.
14. Turner, D., interview, 17 Dec 2013.
15. Ibid.
16. Mullings, J. (Jenny), conversation, 7 Jan 2014.
17. Turner, D., interview, 17 Dec 2013.
18. Ibid.
19. *The House*, Parliament's Weekly Magazine, All-Party Groups, a comprehensive guide, September 2011.
20. *The Times*, register, 5 Mar 2014, p. 52.

## Chapter 8    An extraordinary educational experiment

1.  Turner, D., interview, 23 Dec 2013.
2.  Ibid.
3.  Ibid.
4.  Ibid.
5.  Ibid.
6.  Ibid.
7.  Offord, P., FE Week, 27 Feb 2014.

8. *Lords Hansard, Lord Bilston*, 28 June 2007, Column 719.
9. Ibid.
10. Ibid.
11. *Lords Hansard, Lord Bilston*, 8 May 2008, Column 735.

## Chapter 9    Soft-shoe shuffle into parliament

1. Turner, D., interview, 5 Dec 2013.
2. Ibid.
3. Ibid.
4. Ibid.
5. Ibid.
6. Ibid.
7. Andrew, C.(2009) *The Defence of the Realm*, The Authorised History of M15, Allen Lane, London.
8. Turner, D., interview, 9 Dec 2013.
9. Kinnock, Lord (kinnockn), email, 15 Jan 2014.
10. Lawrence, Dr R., 12 Feb 2014.
11. McFadden, P. (patrick.mcfadden.mp), email, 16 Jan 2014.
12. Lawrence, Dr R., 12 Feb 2014.

## Chapter 10    Steel Man grapples with Iron Lady

1. Wainwright, D., Express & Star, 26 Feb 2014, p. 19.
2. Kavanagh, D., Lord Bilston obituary, *The Guardian*, 27 Feb 2014, p. 33.)
3. Turner, D., interview, 23 Jan 2014.
4. Clelland, D., interview, 3 Feb 2014.
5. Turner, D., interview, 6 Feb 2014.
6. Hansard, H C Debate, 20 July 1987, Vol.118, Column 698-700, 8.05pm.
7. Grocott, B., telephone call, 2 Jan 2014.
8. Hansard, H C Debate, 20 July 1987, Vol.118, Column 698-700, 8.05pm

9.  Ibid.
10. Ibid.
11. Turner, D., interview, 24 Dec 2013.
12. Davies, H., email, 14 Feb 2014.
13. Withers, J., letter, 12 Feb 2014.
14. Turner, D., interview, 24 Dec 2013.
15. Withers, J., letter, 12 Feb 2014.
16. Davies, H., email, 14 Feb 2014.
17. Ibid.
18. Turner, D., interview, 17 Dec 2013.
19. Turner, D., interview, 7 Jan 2014.
20. Turner, T.H. (Bert), interview, 7 Jan 2014.
21. *Lords Hansard* question, 14 June 2011, Column 655.
22. Turner, D., interview, 13 Dec 2013.
23. *F E Week*, 27 Feb 2014.
24. Turner, D., interview, 13 Dec 2013.
25. Ibid.
26. The House, Parliament's Weekly Magazine, All-Party Groups, a comprehensive guide, September 2011.
27. Ibid.
28. Ibid.
29. Turner, D., interview, 3 Feb 2014.
30. Ibid.

## Chapter 11   International development and fair trade

1.  Turner, D., interview, 13 Dec 2013.
2.  Kavanagh, D., Lord Bilston obituary, *The Guardian*, 27 Feb 2014, p. 33.
3.  Turner, D., interview, 13 Dec 2013.
4.  Ibid.
5.  Ibid.
6.  Turner, D., interview, 28 Dec 2013.
7.  Ibid.

8.  Turner, D., interview, 9 Dec 2013.
9.  Ibid.
10. Ibid.
11. *Express & Star*, 12 March 2014.
12. Turner, D., interview, 9 Dec 2013.
13. Alfie, B. Gwinnett's grandson, letter, 14 Jan 2014.
14. Turner, D. & P., interview, 3 Jan 2014.
15. Clelland, D., email, 4 Feb 2014.
16. Turner, D., interview, 9 Dec 2013.
17. Chevannes, M., memory, 3 Jan 2014.
18. McFadden, P. (patrick.mcfadden.mp), email, 16 Jan 2014.
19. Lawrence, Dr R., 12 Feb 2014.

**Chapter 12    Friends in high places**

1.  Turner, D., interview, 28 Dec 2013.
2.  Ibid.
3.  Ibid.
4.  Clelland, D., email, 4 Feb 2014.
5.  Grocott, B., telephone conversation, 2 Jan 2014.
6.  Grocott, B. telephone call & email, 3 Feb 2014.

**Chapter 13    Remoulded nearer to the heart's desire**

1.  *Lords Hansard, Lord Bilston*, 14 July 2005, Column 1289.
2.  Ibid.
3.  Turner, D., interview, 30 Dec 2013.
4.  Turner, T.H. (Bert), interview, 7 Jan 2014.
5.  Cole, N., conversation, email correspondence, Craft Gallery visit, 7 Jan 2014.
6.  Turner, T.H. (Bert), interview, 7 Jan 2014; Bilston Craft Gallery exhibits, 2014.
7.  Bilston Craft Gallery exhibits, 2014
8.  Turner, P. (Pat), interview, 7 Jan 2014; Reeves, F., memory,

2 Jan 2014.
9. Turner, D., interview, 7 Jan 2014.
10. Ibid.
11. Ibid.
12. Lawrence, Dr R., 12 Feb 2014.
13. *Wolverhampton Chronicle*, Stephen Taylor, 20 April 1966.
14. *Express & Star*, 18 Dec 1999.
15. Ibid.
16. Ibid.
17. Ibid.
18. Ibid.

## Chapter 14    Beer lovers' champion

1. Turner, D., interview, 13 Dec 2013.
2. Hansard. Vol 296, Column 348, 18 June 1997.
3. Ibid.
4. Turner, D., interview, 17 Dec 2013.
5. Ibid; and a labelled bottle of the said Dennis Ale.
6. *The House*, Parliament's Weekly Magazine, All-Party Groups, a comprehensive guide, September 2011.
7. Turner, D., interview, 23 Jan 2014.

## Chapter 15    The bold Baron Bilston

1. Turner, D., interview, 27 Dec 2013.
2. Ibid.
3. Ibid.
4. Turner, D., Royal Shrewsbury Hospital, early Dec 2013.
5. Turner, D. and Turner, P., conversation, 27 Dec 2013.
6. Barnsby, G., Barnsby Blog, 'Objection to the proposed installation of Lord Dennis Turner of Bilston as freeman of Wolverhampton', 27 Nov 2006.
7. Turner, D., interview, 24 Dec 2013.

8. Ibid.
9. Ibid.
10. *Lords Hansard*, 3 December 2012, Columns 443– 454, 3 Dec 2012.
11. Ibid.
12. Turner, D., interview, 24 Dec 2013.

## Chapter 16    Till we have built Jerusalem

1. Lawrence, Dr R., 12 Feb 2014.
13. Turner, D., interview, 24 Dec 2013.
14. Ibid.
15. Turner, D., interview, 26 Dec 2013.
16. Hansard, H C Debate, 2 July 1987, Vol 118, Column 698-700, 8.05pm.
17. Turner, D., interview, 24 Dec 2013.
18. Ibid.

## Chapter 17    Out of darkness cometh light

1. Rawnsley, A., email, 29 Jan 2014.
2. Turner, D., interview, 13 Dec 2013.
3. Turner, D., interview, 24 Dec 2013.
4. Lawrence, Dr R., email, 12 Feb 2014.
5. Claymore, I., interview, 20 Jan 2014.
6. Chevannes, M., memory, 3 Feb 2014.
7. *Express & Star*, 26 Feb 2014, First, p. 1.
8. Blair, T., email, 21 Jan 2014.
9. Kinnock, Lord (kinnockn), email, 15 Jan 2014.
10. Miliband, E., letter, 27 Jan 2014.
11. Grocott, B., telephone call & email, 3 Feb 2014.
12. Clelland, D., interview, 3 Feb 2014.
13. Skinner, D., get-well card, Jan 2014.
14. Purchase, K., interview, 2 Jan 2014.
15. McFadden, P. (patrick.mcfadden.mp), email, 6 Jan 2014.

Project facilitator:   Freda Edwards
Format and design:  Sarah Moss Designs Ltd

All proceeds from the sale of this book will go to the
Compton Hospice,
4 Compton Road West,
Wolverhampton WV3 9DH.

Registered Charity No. 512387